BUSTING
SILOS

HOW SNOWFLAKE UNITES SALES AND MARKETING TO WIN ITS BEST CUSTOMERS

BY

HILLARY CARPIO AND TRAVIS HENRY

FOREWORD BY **DENISE PERSSON**, CMO
AND **CHRIS DEGNAN**, CRO, SNOWFLAKE

PEAKPOINT
— PRESS —

Peakpoint Press books may be purchased in bulk at special discounts for sales promotion, corporate gifts, fund-raising, or educational purposes. Special editions can also be created to specifications. For details, contact the Special Sales Department, Skyhorse Publishing, 307 West 36th Street, 11th Floor, New York, NY 10018 or info@skyhorsepublishing.com.

Peakpoint Press® is a registered trademark of
Skyhorse Publishing, Inc.®, a Delaware corporation.

Visit our website at wwww.peakpointpress.com.

10 9 8 7 6 5 4 3 2 1

Library of Congress Cataloging-in-Publication Data is available on file.

Cover design by Francis Mao

ISBN: 978-1-5107-7789-7
Ebook ISBN: 978-1-5107-7790-3

Printed in the United States of America

To our families, mentors, and the Snowflake team
for inspiring and supporting us

Contents

PART 4: SCALE

Foreword
Unprecedented Growth through Extraordinary Alignment

by Denise Persson, chief marketing officer, Snowflake, and Chris Degnan, chief revenue officer, Snowflake

Snowflake is an extraordinary company, and the alignment we have across our company has been a big contributor to our success.

Sales and marketing misalignment is a known issue at many companies. Some corporate leaders even believe that promoting tension between these two departments is beneficial and that it drives healthy competition or motivates top performance. We think that mindset is completely counterproductive. It simply does not work. We're frankly astonished that anyone in the business world still clings to the belief that sales and marketing can operate in silos, much less that they should be intentionally pitted against each other.

When Chris first arrived at Snowflake, he remembers burning through an immense amount of mental energy establishing new processes. All he really wanted to do was get out there and sell, but he couldn't do that without any client meetings. After Denise was hired, she made it clear that sales would be the marketing group's number one customer moving forward. She said her job was to understand his needs and ensure they were met so their joint efforts would build pipeline for Snowflake.

We agreed that all of our activities had to ladder up to growth, revenue, and pipeline. And everything else followed from that agreement.

The success we've had with our teams stems from unity and trust. From the very start, we've created a culture at Snowflake that views sales and marketing as one big collaborative, cooperative supergroup that builds pipeline and drives revenue. We've busted silos that exist elsewhere, and created the greatest growth machine in the business, capturing logos including Capital One, Under Armour, PepsiCo, and JetBlue.

Everything you're about to read in the pages that follow will help you do the same at your own organization. But before you start that journey, we want to offer you some advice from our perspective as passionate silo-busters.

A productive partnership between sales and marketing starts with a positive relationship between both leaders. If there's friction at the leadership level, that friction will trickle down through teams and infect every aspect of the work. We know that some of you reading may be founders, or C-level execs, or emerging leaders, so your ability to control this alignment may vary. But it must be said that what we're doing at Snowflake is fueled by the respect we hold for each other across all functions of our organization. We are business partners who have each other's backs, and everyone knows it. That strengthens everything our teams believe, communicate, and execute.

To achieve insane alignment between sales and marketing, a key value pillar here at Snowflake, you must first focus on trust. All functional organizations are built on trust. Leaders at any level of either group can work toward getting the basics down, capturing and showing consistent results, and establishing their teams as reliable executors. Doing this lays groundwork for a meaningful partnership to grow.

Of course, that partnership will be meaningless if you don't agree that the goal of marketing is to help make selling easier and creating opportunities, and the goal of sales is to turn those opportunities into revenue.

The current marketing teams know that if they aren't putting sales first, they're missing the entire point of their work. It's not that marketing is secondary to sales, but that sales is closer to the customer and revenue and therefore marketing priorities stem from that proximity. Also Denise believes that marketing is all about eliminating waste. When marketing does something that doesn't even have any impact on the sales process, that's the most wasteful use of resources imaginable, and she has no tolerance for it.

For his part, Chris takes Denise's input seriously and collaborates with her on everything from quarterly goals to board presentations. His team is trained to communicate frequently and respectfully with hers, and view all of marketing as valued partners.

This type of ongoing partnership requires honesty and humility. Everyone involved across both organizations needs to leave their egos at the door and be willing to listen. All of our team members know this. They know that they're working for one of the greatest technology companies on the planet and that the tech world is accelerating. If they want to be part of that acceleration, they've got to get on board.

They've got to bust silos, get aligned, and trust each other.

Hillary Carpio and Travis Henry, the authors of this book, have been consistent champions of this philosophy, and this book is bursting with their insights into making it work. As wildly effective leaders in account-based marketing (ABM) and sales development (SDR) work, respectively, they've proven that marketing and sales teams can go farther and faster when they link arms. As pragmatists, they've taught their people that waste is unacceptable and all their work should be traced back to revenue generation. And as mentors, consultants, and advisers they've trained the next generation of marketing and sales leaders to think of everyone across both orgs as part of one big team.

And the book they've created is an actionable handbook for building your own end-to-end pipeline-generation machine on a foundation of radical alignment. As you read it, you'll see how to unlock brand-new possibilities once you establish that alignment. Every chapter illustrates why alignment is so impactful, shows you what you can build with that alignment, explains how to activate what you've built, and offers advice on how to scale it up.

Read on to find out how they did all this at startup speed and enterprise scale, and steal their secrets for yourself. They will take you from scrappy first experiments where you can afford to fail fast without risking your neck, to scaled-up programs with global reach and an immense amount of automation.

And take it from us: the quickest route to extraordinary growth is creating extraordinary alignment between sales and marketing.

Introduction
Wide Nets and Wasted Resources

Although it only operated for a little more than eighteen months between 1860 and 1861, the Pony Express transformed how Americans communicated. This now-legendary system drastically cut the time it took to send mail between the east and west coasts of the United States, sometimes by a factor of six. Instead of loading envelopes onto hulking ships or lumbering stagecoaches, messages were carried by individual couriers moving swiftly on horseback through a series of checkpoints between Missouri to California. Riders hot-swapped from fatigued horses to fresh ones to maximize speed, stopping only for their own rest and caloric intake.

The Pony Express achieved a stepwise advance in communications velocity and reliability by stitching together a coordinated set of motions that worked continuously under very specific circumstances. If one of the waypoints wasn't ready to supply the rider with a fresh horse, or if the waypoints were spread out beyond a day's ride, the entire system would break down. The riders themselves even had to stay under a weight limit of 125 pounds. The horses they chose were specialized for stamina and distance. Before being supplanted by the telegraph, this system worked to reduce the average mail delivery time from coast to coast from multiple months to a ten-day sprint, from sender to recipient.

Cultivating new business isn't all that different. To achieve real efficacy in today's B2B sales and marketing landscape, you must orchestrate a symphony of content, digital experiences, peer validation, physical mail, in-person events, and the all-important human touch points of live conversations and asynchronous messages. And you need to do that at the scale of thousands of unique businesses and tens of thousands of unique humans in those businesses, with each permutation demanding a resonant value proposition that compels action.

Generating new business takes follow-through, vigilance, and skill, and it's not something that can ever stop. As individuals who have dedicated our careers to growing B2B revenue as leaders, operators, advisers, and consultants for dozens of companies, we've learned the prospecting motion must be continuous and unbroken. Inbound leads must be triaged in a timely manner; outbound motions need room to build on themselves over weeks and months; and signals from target accounts can present themselves at any time and vanish just as quickly. Sales teams can't focus exclusively at closing business in the immediate quarter; if they do, they wake up on day one of the next quarter inside a forecasting hole.

The hardest part of closing a deal is finding it. So we must always be looking.

At Snowflake, one of our mantras is "target the right accounts at the right time with the right message to the right people." Doing this involves complex orchestration and organizational alignment that no single team can create alone. But any team or individual can start the work of alignment at a small scale and build a solid case.

Lessons from our past roles and the framework we've constructed at Snowflake have helped us amplify that effort. We've built systems that enable us to address accounts, timing, messaging, and people simultaneously, as have many other corporations. What sets us apart is our ability to do these things in a highly targeted, one-to-one way as well as a digitally enabled at-scale approach, all while working as one big unified team.

Everyone wants to target the right accounts at the right time and deliver the right message to the right people. In this book, we'll talk about how to *actually* do it, from ideation to execution, at startup speed and enterprise scale.

We know how because we've done it. We've created new systems and augmented existing ones to keep the Snowflake sales pipeline full at all times. We've either been in your shoes ourselves or worked with incredible people in your shoes. We know what it's like to stare down a broken strategy and know it can be made better.

We also understand the temptation to solve go-to-market (GTM) problems by paying an expert consultant to come in and make those problems go away. We've even been those consultants. So we know the truth: Real change can and should be driven by tackling the tough work of internal alignment across your GTM teams. What we are proposing in this book is an evolution that builds on the concept of account-based, the strategy where marketing focuses on a specific set of accounts with tailored messaging and content. We will walk you through how to bring your revenue teams together to amplify your impact and ramp up your growth curve. We call this coming together of marketing, sales, and sales development "one-team go-to-market (GTM)."

All this to say that we're speaking from experience. (Including dealing with our fair share of failures.) Both of us have driven change in pipeline-generation philosophies and processes for many years. And in the case of our work at Snowflake, we've had the opportunity to build an orchestrated one-team GTM machine that effectively engages the largest organizations in the world and maximizes the odds of landing them as customers. Undoubtedly, we have benefited from the work of predecessors, colleagues, market timing, and an unbelievable product. But we have also worked through the challenges of alignment and pushed the boundaries of what is possible in today's data-driven, technology-enabled world of sales and marketing.

Here's how it all got started.

A meeting of aligned minds

Hillary was working as a marketing manager at a network security company. Her job was to take a suite of solutions across the organization and develop GTM campaigns that included touch points from all marketing teams including corporate communications, product marketing, digital marketing, content marketing, and the web team. The company was close to mastering the bill of materials for the one-to-many approach, with well-aligned content, messaging, and delivery. The problem was that despite how well-oiled the machine seemed to be, it wasn't netting the highest-profile, highest-spending customers. Hillary's team needed to narrow their focus and make an impact on a list of key accounts selected by leadership. Doing this would help the company hit their overall revenue targets.

Because she's constantly hunting for process improvements and ways to connect cross-functional teams, Hillary attended a conference, learned how Snowflake did account-based marketing (ABM), and brought those ideas back to her employer . . . with a twist. She had developed a reputation for stitching together free and existing technology to expand her impact beyond single-human limitations, and that's what she did here. She took what she'd learned from Snowflake—which had a five-person team—and applied it as a one-person team by using tech to scale. Since the learnings were designed for a resourced team of multiple people, Hillary modified them and tweaked them to use as a foundation for what she wanted to do, and built her own ideas on top of them. (A practice we'll strongly encourage you to do throughout this book.) This included pitching to the sales development (SDR) team to ask for volunteers to participate, and hiring developers out of Romania for $2K to help her connect a few key pieces in her tech stack.

She built up her ABM practice and refined it. Now able to target thousands of accounts with relevant messaging and content—with a subset of those messages teed up for SDR outreach as a team—she had results within a few weeks showing a 122 percent increase in SDR open rates, fifteen times the industry standard meeting conversion rate, and a sevenfold increase in reply rates. At this point she and her manager, the VP of corporate marketing, brand and demand at her company, knew they were onto something. By joining forces with the SDR function, they had cracked the code for taking their existing campaign infrastructure, tailoring it to top accounts, and scaling it. She proved that an account-based approach could be launched successfully, regardless of resources. It just required an innovative mindset and bias toward action.

Snowflake's ABM experts heard about her innovations and got in touch with her. Inspired by the opportunities available at Snowflake, she later made the leap to lead its ABM function into the next era of the company's scale, to IPO and beyond. In her new role, her first priority was to fortify and maximize the relationships between ABM folks and SDRs within the company. Although Snowflake was a big, well-funded organization with existing ABM, sales, and SDR departments and enthusiastic support from leadership, Hillary saw an opportunity to truly unify these teams.

She approached the SDR team with a grand plan of how they could collaborate to prioritize their accounts using intent data, then roll out an end-to-end program. But together they recognized that her grand plan was too grand, and she needed to scale back and look for one small way they could work together to get the ball rolling.

Instead of using intent data to orchestrate outreach to thousands of accounts, they took one person on Hillary's ABM team and equipped them with the right data to partner with an SDR on a list of about ten accounts. This right-sized partnership worked spectacularly, and Hillary began making plans to scale her efforts slowly and methodically. Even with leadership buy-in and a solid vision, change takes time and requires winning the hearts and minds of cross-functional teams.

Meanwhile, Travis had been working in marketing and sales development roles for his whole career, and saw a repeating pattern of go-to-market inefficiency at the companies he worked at and consulted for. Marketing generated huge demand at great cost, but had little insight into and direction regarding what was happening with that demand. Often conversations with marketing leaders would circle back to the same script. There was lots of focus on what the company could do to optimize its campaigns, increase engagement, and drive more leads from the marketing dollars being spent, but Travis saw that these were the wrong issues to focus on, akin to Henry Ford focusing on smithing better horseshoes. Meanwhile, sales teams would regularly pursue the long, difficult road of cold outbound prospecting to individuals who had never been exposed to the company's value proposition. Nobody was dedicated to and bought into converting the demand that marketing was producing into the things that mattered to the business: meetings, opportunities, and revenue.

This led him to recognize the power of the sales development representative (SDR) role. But that also wasn't enough. SDRs themselves were not effective without the direction and guidance of the sales team, who held ultimate responsibility for the accounts that we were all trying to get in front of. He knew that inviting prospects to show up at an event, mingle with their peers, nosh on a scone, and learn about the company's value proposition was necessary, but not sufficient in creating customers. These marketing campaigns had to be paired with a formalized sales follow-up mechanism to get prospects to a real buying cycle.

Finding and understanding the SDR function—a specialized role that sits between the scone and the sale—was a breakthrough for him. But his real aha moment came when he saw the power of a well-engineered tech stack in the hands of these purpose-built prospectors. He realized that the output of a single SDR could be multiplied by five to ten times if that person had clean data, the ability to automate the mundane, and a tight interlock with buying signals that they could home in on. So Travis pioneered the function of dedicated Sales Development Operations and Enablement, bringing the strategy and process rigor usually reserved for quota-carrying sales teams to the demand creating SDR teams at the top of the funnel. SDRs are one of the most data-driven, process-oriented, and tool-enabled functions in a go-to-market team, yet most companies do not dedicate an operations professional (or team) to support them. Travis was brought into Snowflake as an operations leader to shepherd the function's growth from a group of 85 to more than 250 individuals.

Once the two of us started talking, we knew we were on the same page. And we were able to hit the ground running because the basic foundation was in place. Snowflake already had sales reps assigned to a list of accounts, ABM was already being used (though not in the way we were envisioning), and leadership had already put an SDR team in place. All of these factors helped us, as did identifying each other as like minds. Hillary had already been getting her team in place and pitching her ideas, but when Travis joined Snowflake it was like a door had opened for us both, and we could walk through it together.

At first, it was just the two of us putting our minds together, brainstorming how we could initiate change at a small scale within the larger company. Both of us had done similar work outside Snowflake with fewer resources and at smaller companies, so we were well positioned to build on our experiences. Now we have the same grassroots mentality but with stellar teams to support us and massive scale to push us. By creating some early wins together, gathering momentum among open-minded team members, landing some big clients using our strategies, and eventually making the case to leadership that our one-team GTM operation merited ongoing investment, we've built one of the largest teams in the industry.

If we can get started with just two people—two believers in the ABM way and the importance of aligning sales with marketing—so can you.

And honestly? If you find the right coconspirators, you can get a lean little ABM, sales, and SDR machine up and running in about three months, with whichever mix of resources you have. Most of the strategies we're about to explain can be enacted with a few eager people and a creative plan to connect existing tech in a smarter way.

How This Book Works

Our job is to help you find your collaborators, experiment with some plays, and decide if this way of working works for you. We know you're perusing these pages now so you can learn Snowflake's one-team GTM secrets and apply them inside your own company. And we're genuinely excited to share those secrets with you! One-team GTM is a journey, and not always a linear one. We wrote this book expecting that some of you will be intimately familiar with some of the concepts we explore and will thumb through them to dive into the nitty-gritty of execution; others will appreciate a full-spectrum guide from ideation to measurement. We hope you'll bookmark, highlight, and use this book as a field guide through your journey. The fact that you picked up a copy in the first place proves that you believe there's a better, more efficient way to pilot a twenty-first-century sales and marketing operation. You're our kind of people, and we know you can succeed.

We wrote this book because we've been where you may be now, discovered (through real trial and error) how powerful an account-based strategy can be, and figured out how to move from loose idea to cold, hard execution.

We also wrote this book because we really, truly want to help you go to market more efficiently and effectively. We want to help you build your own Pony Express for your pipeline, and fundamentally transform your GTM processes. We are both process-savvy, operationally minded doers who make the most of whatever resources we've got, and it kills us to know that most sales and marketing departments still spend their time working against each other rather than cooperating. We might not be able to change that dynamic everywhere all at once but, with your help, we can start a groundswell. We can start convincing people that there's a better, more engaging, more profitable way to do business. And that way is *together*.

That said, this book is not an HR manual. We won't be teaching you how to pitch an organizational change to your board or navigate the most toxic personalities in your company. You'll have to manage those interpersonal politics on your own. We also won't be offering solutions for lack of product fit, or ways to save a sinking ship. Uniting sales and marketing through a one-team approach is a long play, not a last-ditch effort.

This book is for you if you're a doer, an ambitious tactician, a person who wants to make a positive impact regardless of your position in the org chart. The learnings and guidance we've compiled in these pages span from strategic plans down to gritty tactical details.

We've also structured the book in such a way that you can learn how to build a world-class GTM machine from scratch or skip past topics you've already mastered to level up your operation. In short, we wrote this book for B2B go-to-market leaders of all levels who are looking for a better way to grow revenue.

In part 1, we'll help you build a custom on-ramp to merging sales and marketing and creating your own pipeline-generating machinery at startup speed. While we heartily agree with Snowflake CEO Frank Slootman that "execution beats strategy every day of the week," the truth is that you'll set up your account-based program to fail without a solid understanding of what you're trying to achieve. The chapters in this part of the book will challenge your thinking about why your business should change and who should be involved in the conversation.

Then in part 2 we show you how to get the structures, knowledge, and content in place to fuel that machine. These chapters will help you get a clear picture of which customers you want to bring into the fold and get you building the mechanisms you need to grab their attention.

Part 3 dives straight into defining and running your first big plays. We will cover the necessity of great timing and how to solve for it, stitching your content together, and drawing clear swim lanes for your GTM teams to bring everything to life for your target customers.

And finally in part 4, we walk you through the path to enterprise scale. We will explain how you can ramp up your marketing offers and seamlessly present them to thousands of companies instead of dozens. You will also get a sneak peek at how we see data powering the future of revenue.

Nearly every chapter wraps up with a table highlighting what you'll need to do to create a "minimum viable" or "scaled" version of the processes we've explained. It also summarizes some mistakes to avoid as you dive into execution.

As you make your way through these pages, we'll give you a bit of advice, plenty of strategies, and a handful of perspectives besides ours so you can see how this marketing magic works inside Snowflake itself. We'll also share insights from our work with other B2B startups and scale-ups. Our hope is that you'll highlight your favorite passages and dog-ear a few pages so you can refer back to ideas you're eager to implement.

We're not promising to change your business overnight, but we believe with these tools and ideas you could get to your first one-team GTM "win" in as little as a few weeks, changing the trajectory of your go-to-market machine over the next eight to twelve months.

It's gonna be a wild ride. Are you ready? Let's go.

PART 1
WHY

1

Do the Unthinkable: Marry Sales and Marketing

When a big, sophisticated buyer considers making a purchase, many teams need to work together to enable the sale. We know this because we've been involved in closing deals with some of the biggest logos in the business world, including multinational corporations on the Global 2000 list. We're fortunate to count several of the most complex and multifaceted media and entertainment companies ever to have existed as our clients.

Like many multinational corporations on the Global 2000 list, media companies are complicated to sell into for B2B tech orgs like ours. Most are actually composed of multiple, disparate companies including movie, television, and gaming studios, TV channels, news networks, and music houses. On top of that complexity, these corporations pose other sales challenges, including:

Employment of global teams and execution of regional initiatives

Frequent acquisitions, mergers, and joint ventures

Use of legacy technology cobbled together with newer offerings

The complications created by executive turnover and evolving vision

Disconnected buying cycles that create an excess of resources

For us at Snowflake, media companies present a massive opportunity, but no one salesperson can take it on alone. We have a whole team dedicated to selling into a few of our most prominent media clients, comprising one global account manager, two account executives, one territory account manager, one sales development representative, three sales engineers, and three professional services folks. These people only support selling initiatives for a single, high-priority company. They work on no other accounts.

Our sales and marketing strategy is designed to be multifaceted and address the needs of each of the biggest organizational sectors within the company. Our sales team starts by splitting the account and prioritizing different segments based on account intelligence.

Big, sophisticated buyers require a big, sophisticated approach.

And once we become part of the infrastructure, we are often able to do some silo busting *within the walls of our client companies*. Since Snowflake helps organizations centralize, organize, share, and better leverage their data and assets, we've been able to convince some of our Global 2000 clients—slowly, diplomatically, and in ways that genuinely serve them—to collaborate across their own teams and units. We offer webinars and trainings, show them how to share valuable insights across the business, and help them solve their business problems by improving their internal communication. We have entire teams of people dedicated to serving single clients as one team, and supporting their clients across all stages of the sales cycle.

We net and keep global enterprise customers because we are dedicated to learning about their needs, fulfilling those needs, and adapting to meet any new needs that might arise.

We net and keep global enterprise customers because we serve them as a unified team.

To state the obvious, Snowflake would never be able to land a single subsidiary within a global media enterprise using a wide net. Even a spearfishing approach—semi-targeted marketing efforts that reached a handful of mid-level leaders—probably would've fallen flat. Sophisticated, global buyers require a truly personalized buying experience. We had to sharpen our harpoons to make this happen.

Wide nets aren't exactly obsolete, but they're definitely ill-suited to the current fast-paced, information-flooded marketplace. With all the data, analytics, and tools available right now, we believe that B2B players who aren't hyper-focused on priming and reaching their ideal customers are wasting time and resources. That said, we understand why many brilliant sales teams and marketing groups struggle to do that very thing.

One-Team GTM: The Future of ABM

Account-based marketing (ABM) is the inverse approach to the wide net. As a strategy, ABM has been floating around in one form or another since the 1990s, when companies recognized the need for personalized marketing efforts. Since then it has gone out of style, and then come back into focus as a more efficient way to capture ideal-fit customers.

WHAT IS ACCOUNT-BASED
vs. ABM vs. ONE-TEAM GTM?

Account-Based: We refer to "account-based" as the strategic practice of identifying a set of accounts and executing activities against them. Sales, demand gen, field marketing, SDRs and beyond can all be account-based without being aligned and orchestrating across functions. This is where we see the problem.

ABM: Account-based marketing (ABM) is the marketing team dedicated to executing account-based programs that range from one-to-one to one-to-many.

One-Team GTM: One-team GTM is the unified, scaled strategy and execution of an account-based motion across GTM teams. Which teams are included in this GTM mix will vary based on your org structure, company size, and account-based maturity. The core of this strategy involves sales, sales development, and account-based marketing.

Do not use as: a targeted demand-get effort limited to dynamic, segmented ads at scale without sales input.

How did this resurgence of interest in ABM happen? What changed?

Data became more transparent: Companies now have the ability to identify (almost) every customer they might want to target. Why spend marketing dollars attracting companies who aren't actually a fit for your product?

Recurring revenue models were born: The software as a service (SaaS) industry showed the growth leverage of landing the right customer with a high ceiling for expansion potential. You can now reassure your CFO that these logos are worth spending on if you can land them.

Increased noise drove a desire to differentiate: Marketing automation created a bridge between ABM 1.0 and its revival. As automation tools became common, their effectiveness waned and rekindled the need to "stand out" to buyers.

Buying committees rose to power: Big purchase decisions are now made by groups within companies who need to be engaged as a buying center, not individual decision-makers. In 2022, *Harvard Business Review* described that "Most B2B buyers start their journey by assembling an internal committee, whose members have different roles in influencing the decision. The committee often consists of three tiers: Ultimate approvers who own the decision; a core buying committee that does the research and runs the process; and internal influencers, including end users, who provide comments on vendors and products.

Given all of these shifts, it makes sense that ABM—a strategy that enables marketing and sales to identify, reach, and sign big, desirable customers—is seeing a second wave of popularity. Now, we are in an account-based era where 62 percent of B2B marketers plan to increase their investment in ABM technology in the next year. This approach and the supporting tools are approaching maturity, though still evolving. Now is the perfect time for this way of working to experience a revival.

However, plenty of organizations have resisted revamping their strategies. At this point, most marketers know ABM exists, but many aren't sure how to implement it in their own organizations or industries. This happens for a whole slew of reasons, including:

People don't know where to start. Getting the machinery of ABM up and running seems like an overwhelming task, and even expert marketers may assume they're unqualified to handle it, because it spans multiple teams, multiple marketing tactics, and multiple channels.

Analytics and data can be incredibly overwhelming: Many marketers don't know how to wrangle data and make sense of it. How should they score accounts? How do they analyze data attributes for those accounts in a meaningful way?

Companies assume software is all that's needed: Many companies are buying ABM platforms to tackle this, but find themselves overinvested in technology and still lacking the strategy and executional know-how to leverage it fully. They struggle to translate the buzzword definition of ABM into something meaningful for their business.

Marketers don't feel empowered to bring ABM to fruition: They may be individual contributors or otherwise "low-ranking" employees, so it never occurs to them that they could initiate company-wide change.

On a surface level, ABM may seem tricky to measure: Marketers are scared of failing and don't know what success looks like.

Leaders are worried about the cost: They think it's too expensive or requires hiring a fleet of new people.

They don't have the patience to follow through on ABM: Many marketers (and their bosses) want results *now*, but ABM can take several months (or even quarters) to show ROI.

Alternatively, companies may have harvested gobs of data and analytics from various sources, but have no idea how to put those insights to use. They may even have invested in costly ABM dashboards from third-party vendors to capture and categorize all their customer signals, yet remain paralyzed when it comes to taking meaningful action. Plenty of teams are leveraging multiple ABM-related technologies and strategies without knowing it or without knowing how to optimize them.

Others are actively avoiding the strategy. Marketing and sales leaders may be especially wary if they see ABM as a passing fad. As industry veterans, we've seen lots of frameworks and tools get forced on workers just because they're trendy. In an attempt to stay relevant, companies may invest in tech before fully understanding how to use it or if it truly applies to their needs. Or they may buy software and dashboards as a Hail Mary approach. They buy into the promise that ABM can be done via technology as an all-in-one, without realizing they have to power that tech with their own strategies. Leaders who have lived through these tech-investment nightmares are often leery of buying into new methodologies. They've been burned too many times before.

At the core of all these issues is an all-too-common misunderstanding: *Tools alone can't solve problems. People need to use tools to solve problems.* And lacking people who can both use the tools and navigate the problems, you're sunk. That shiny new dashboard isn't gonna run itself.

Bridging the gap between tools and tool-users isn't as simple as just hiring more bodies. You need people who have bought into the philosophy of targeted prospecting, solid playbooks and strategies, and the collective energy to tackle a whole lot of execution and orchestration. True believers and willing collaborators. As we wrote this book, we mulled the next generation of ABM and considered what to call our approach. There are several terms on the market, such as ABX (account-based everything), ABSD (account-based sales development), and GTM (go to market), but none capture the essence of what makes our approach unique: seamless execution across customer-facing teams. For that reason, we are suggesting to leave acronyms and spin-offs of AB____ behind us and focus on the outcome: A one-team go-to-market approach.

We define one-team GTM as the unified, scaled strategy and execution of an account-based motion across GTM teams.

Counterproductivity Codified

One-team GTM is by its nature an integrated motion. It requires highly surgical demand generation, which marketing is uniquely equipped to provide. But it also requires deep account knowledge and human execution, which is where sales comes in. With that in mind, welcome to square one. Marrying sales and marketing is your critical first step toward building an efficient, effective one-team GTM engine inside your current organization.

And we know it's a doozy.

WHAT IS GTM?

At its core, a go-to-market (GTM) strategy is a plan that outlines how an organization can engage with customers to convince them to buy their product or service.

A well-oiled marketing and sales machine requires contributions from all functions, from brand and PR to sales and operations. Within the broader sales and marketing functions, there are a few specifically geared toward the final mile, the teams executing plays together directly to potential customers. While these can include a variety of team combinations dependent on your organization, we will refer to GTM teams as sales, sales development, and account-based marketing for the purpose of this book. We acknowledge that there are a host of functions that plug into these teams. You can read in chapter 11 how Snowflake works as an even larger GTM team.

As most people working in either group will attest, sales and marketing are often misaligned. In fact, we'd wager they're locking horns right now at scrappy startups and behemoth enterprises alike, across every industry imaginable. We all hate this dynamic, but few of us know how to combat it. And if we don't talk about *why* it's happening, we'll never be able to change it.

Here's our take: Sales and marketing misalignment persists because conventional GTM strategies push these functions apart. And the further apart they drift, the more trust becomes eroded.

In *The Five Dysfunctions of a Team*, Patrick Lencioni examines the dynamics that drive friction inside workplaces, and "absence of trust" is cited as the root cause of team clashes. (The other four essentially use this dysfunction as a launchpad.) He points out that teams who lack trust conceal mistakes, jump to conclusions about the intentions of others, hold grudges, and dread meetings. The way sales and marketing teams are traditionally set up feeds into the natural, foundational dysfunction of trust that Lencioni describes. They are teams that intrinsically know they are responsible for revenue and dependent on one another to some extent, but they are composed of individuals with fundamentally different skill sets and backgrounds. Add in the wrong strategies and definitions of success, allow people on both teams to avoid talking to each other, and mix those factors together in a quarterly pressure cooker of make-or-miss results, and you can see how trust gets eroded.

This is the paradigm we follow simply because it's what our predecessors laid out for us. Sales views marketing as a service agency—plying them with requests for custom-built customer stories and high-design decks—but marketing resists that characterization. Marketing tracks its own KPIs, frequently focusing on MQLs, and often struggles to connect its metrics back to company-wide revenue goals (despite increasing and exceeding their lead target every quarter). Leaders from both worlds butt heads, and their employees assume they should follow suit.

The absolute worst part about sales and marketing remaining locked in a departmental feud? The counterproductivity. In a B2B context, both groups—and all of their subgroups and dependent teams—*exist to grow top-line revenue for the company*. Period. These two teams have the same goal. It's a broad goal, so plenty of wildly varied tasks can fall beneath it, but it's a shared objective, which means that these teams working against each other is equivalent to them working against themselves. Remaining rivals is making all of the work harder for everyone and keeping true success at arm's length.

Collaborating on this shared objective is a street that runs both ways. Just as it's important for marketers to be thought-partners in any collateral or writing they generate, it's important for salespeople to have a say in what qualifies a lead. According to a study by Marketo, companies with aligned sales and marketing teams are 67 percent better at closing deals. Involving sales in the definition of MQLs can help create a more accurate definition that leads to higher quality leads and more closed deals. And with more buyers conducting independent research, 81 percent of sales representatives say collaborating with their marketing counterparts helps them close more deals.[1] They feel more informed and prepared to make their pitches.

Clearly, this is a partnership that can lead to measurable, ongoing success. That doesn't mean it will be easy to tee up.

Fortunately there are technologies, roles, and mindsets that can break the cycle of rivalry, tactics that can quickly and efficiently generate some measurable wins so you can get people talking, drum up support, and launch a guerrilla campaign to start doing things differently.

Who are the players?

Before we dive into tactics for marrying sales and marketing, let's talk roles. If we cornered a handful of marketing practitioners and sales executives and asked them to define their departmental functions, we're quite sure we'd get a spectacularly varied array of answers. So here's a snapshot of our own definitions:

---

1   Gilberd, Adam. "10 New Findings Reveal How Sales Teams Are Achieving Success Now." Salesforce: The 360 Blog. December 8, 2022. https://www.salesforce.com/blog/15-sales-statistics/

We see **marketing** as a team that drives demand by spreading awareness of products and services at a high level. Marketing educates on why to buy.

We see **sales** as a team that is responsible for bringing in revenue and engaging with customers. Sales enables the buying.

The duties that these two teams perform are definitely different, but the overall goal is the same: drive revenue for the business. Both groups exist to communicate with the customer about their needs and pain points and direct them toward purchasable solutions. Both groups do work that is meant to increase sales and drive revenue. This vitally important overlap is what so many sales and marketing teams fail to see or choose to ignore. Part of the problem is that each department defines itself individually in reference to itself, not as part of a collective effort to support sales, buying, and the generation of revenue. We're framing ourselves and our relationships to each other in the wrong ways. As teams, we may be doing different work, but we're driving toward the same objective.

Busting silos starts here: by recognizing the shared goal, redefining everyone's roles to be in alignment with that goal, and committing to the formation of a single, united team.

At Snowflake, we've worked toward conceptualizing sales and marketing as one big team, focused on a shared revenue goal for the next several years. Our shared goal keeps us focused on supporting each other. **That said, we still make this crucial distinction: marketing's work is focused on pipeline generation and sales' work is focused on forecasting revenue.**

In other words, marketing unlocks the ability to fill our pipeline continuously, which enables sales to forecast accurately. At Snowflake, our marketers measure their success and plan their activities based on the health of the sales pipeline. Tending to that pipeline becomes their primary focus. MQLs, conversions, engagement rates, and other traditional metrics don't go away, but they end up serving pipeline coverage and health.

These are two groups of experts doing business-critical work, but that work becomes exponentially more impactful when everyone from both groups starts collaborating.

INSIDE THE IGLOO WITH SNOWFLAKE:

Lars Christensen, vice president of marketing and demand generation at Snowflake, on how ABM and SDRs unlock sales and marketing alignment

A seasoned B2B marketer with more than eighteen years of experience in growth marketing for leading software companies, Lars Christensen has been Snowflake's vice president of demand generation since 2016 and has nearly two decades of experience in growth marketing for leading software companies. He has a proven track record of developing integrated and impactful demand-generation campaigns that have significantly improved company revenue. Originally from Denmark, Lars currently resides in the Bay Area.

We asked him to speak about the importance of creating and maintaining alignment between marketing and sales teams, and how he influenced that dynamic here at Snowflake.

In the world of B2B marketing, we traditionally relied on lead waterfalls to show what we were accomplishing. We'd present those to sales, showing them, "Here are the total leads, then the accepted leads, then the qualified leads," and so on. I think that was a perfectly decent system, except for the fact that leads are not that interesting for sales. Their language is accounts. They want to know exactly what marketing has done for them within each of their accounts. This is one of the reasons I chose to champion ABM within Snowflake.

ABM allows us to get that kind of clarity much more easily. First it gives us more tools for tracking and showing activity within accounts. We have reporting, we have tactics and motions, where we can go in as tight as we want all the way down to the individual level, and we can explain to each salesperson what we did for their accounts this quarter.

But adopting ABM also allowed us to shift our mindsets around success. We began to define marketing and marketing success in terms of how we were able to create engagement in those accounts. Instead of creating our own goals in a vacuum, we began meeting with salespeople to say, "Let's discuss what you need done in the twenty accounts that you own." And we'd find out that some of them need a first meeting, some of them need pipeline acceleration, some of them need a cross-sell to be introduced into another functional area. We got them to describe that for us. And then we took that information and acted on it. We used ABM tactics and SDR motions to get them the meeting, the acceleration, the introduction to that other functional area, whatever they needed.

The ABM strategy just spoke to sales in a way that I've never really seen before. It allowed marketing to connect with sales in new ways. We could never have gotten sales excited about ABM unless we went in saying, "We are committed to doing this for a relatively large cross-section of the accounts that you own." So we said exactly that.

And you can't get the ABM motion right unless you also have the SDR motion, so we made that a priority, too. On the SDR side of the equation, aligning sales and marketing helps with efficiency, trust-building, and increased clarity.

Here's what I mean by that: If you ask one hundred account executives, they will have one hundred different opinions about what an SDR team is supposed to be doing. Everything from doing contact discovery to event registration to meeting prep and meeting research. And in a lot of companies, that is exactly what has been happening. The alignment into sales has been so strong that individual SDR success depends almost exclusively on feedback from the AEs they're servicing. SDRs had to do anything and everything their AEs asked of them, and it became insanely difficult to measure exactly any outcomes. The SDR services provided back to the sales organization became such a hodgepodge. You can't know whether an SDR motion was successful or not if you need to look across one hundred SDRs who are all providing a mix of services that are all measured in different ways.

When we made the decision that the SDRs should begin reporting into marketing, that changed the dynamic, because SDR work became an extension of the prospecting motions that marketing is putting into play. Because of the reporting structure, we could create some governance around what the SDR team could do and could not do. It may have felt restrictive to sales at first, but in the end they saw that we were better able to serve their accounts, show what we'd done for them, and explain what was successful. I think it's easier to provide that level of governance if the SDRs are reporting into marketing.

There's so much great technology out there and I'm excited to help open people's eyes to what's truly possible right now. Especially with the right organizational alignment.

Find Your Allies and Ask Some Questions

Given the tradition of mistrust between sales and marketing, we recommend approaching the marriage of these teams in terms of efficiency. Regardless of which department you work for, the best possible argument for merging into a single team is this: It will make everyone's work more effective and efficient. You can accomplish more together than you can separately.

One way to frame this is to start poking at your current measurements of success. Ask your colleagues, "Is what we're doing now actually working? How could we make it more effective?" If "number of qualified leads" is your current success measurement, would it be better to follow those leads further down the funnel? We're not suggesting that you invite everyone from both teams to hash it out in a single session. Kick around these ideas with colleagues you like and trust, and do so casually. Plant the seeds by asking people to share their views. Begin the work of resetting expectations on both sides. It doesn't have to be an entire overhaul from the start.

Here's an example from our own playbooks: Hillary meets regularly with marketing and sales leaders at Snowflake and asks them, "What is your goal for this quarter? What are you hearing from customers? What is keeping you up at night?" She uses these as jumping-off points to dive into how her team can help them reach their goals, as opposed to dumping marketing-led initiatives on them.

Then, with some initial data gathered, look for an ally. Someone on the other side with an open mind and a willingness to lead productive changes. Who is most open to this idea on the other team? Who might enjoy talking about this new way of working? Who is closest to the customer and may be eager to find ways to serve that customer better?

You don't need to pair up with someone in a particular role or at a specific level in the org chart. You need to identify someone with passion and talent: someone who matches your own incessant need for innovation, deep curiosity, and desire to build something new. It needs to be a person who's interested in how things work and ready to help change existing systems for the better.

As you search for this person, keep an open mind. You may actually find your best allies in unlikely spots. You might not think to start with a sales development representative who is a new hire with relatively little authority inside your organization. You might not consider field marketers, since they don't run broader campaigns and don't typically have a digital budget. Yet field marketing is one of our best allies at Snowflake. People in these roles (and others) could have the dedication, skills, and grit you need to make real headway together.

Once you've got your ally in mind, consider how best to build the relationship. We strongly recommend doing it through openness, curiosity, asking questions, and focusing on shared outcomes. Making demands or telling people "how it ought to be done" seldom builds trust. Showing genuine interest in their ideas, needs, and perspectives is a far better way to build bridges.

If you are in sales: You may be used to chatting with marketing when you need a pitch deck or email template, but you'll need to approach this conversation differently. In order to establish trust (which you currently lack), you need to understand how you can add value to each other's bottom lines. You need to connect at a strategic level. In order to do that, here are some questions to ask:

> Would you be willing to talk about what my forecast looks like for the quarter? I'd love your support on firming up some soft spots in my pipeline coverage.

> Do you feel like the way we're currently collaborating is working? Are our measures of success lining up?

I've been reading about account-based marketing, and am really intrigued. Do you know much about it?

What do you see working with other regions that we can replicate?

If you are in marketing: You may not be used to reaching out to sales at all, and you can certainly wait until they come to you to reframe an ask. (A salesperson asks for a pitch deck and you say, "Totally! But I'd also love to talk about your overall goals. There might be other ways my team could partner with you strategically.") But if you're ready to make the first move, here are some suggestions:

I was wondering if we could try something new. Instead of asking you how many leads you need, can you tell me about your goals? Do you think what we're doing now is getting us to those goals?

I've been reading about an account-based approach, and I feel like it might work well for our teams. Do you know much about it?

Would you be interested in setting a revenue goal together? I'd love to partner and see what we could accomplish together.

Asking these questions takes some real courage, because they represent big mindset shifts for many people. In fact, you may look at these suggestions and feel like they'll be too overwhelming for you as the messenger, and too zoomed out for anyone on the receiving end of your message. If that's the case, trust your gut, but also consider collaborating on something tactical. Instead of approaching your ally via a weighty conversation about goals and processes, approach them with a small, quick-and-easy experiment you can run together.

Collaborate to Net a Small Win

You've found your ally, and you've had a couple of casual, groundwork-laying conversations. You know you're on the same page, because you both believe that sales and marketing should be working together instead of in opposition. What now? You're not ready to approach leadership and propose org chart changes, not by a long shot. So how can you keep the momentum and excitement going?

As your next step toward alignment, consider finding easy, low-stakes ways to collaborate. If you and your partner can do something together and show positive results, no matter how small, you've taken a step in the right direction.

For the two of us, this meant collaborating on some LinkedIn ads.

Hillary's team was running targeted advertisements on LinkedIn, and they were generating interest in Snowflake's offerings, but no one had direct follow-through planned. Travis suggested they work together on a quick play that the sales development representatives (SDRs) could execute: reaching out to people who had clicked on, commented on, or liked the ads, and following up with them. Within two weeks, we were booking meetings from those ad engagements. This started as a manual process, but once we'd gotten the hang of it, we found ways to automate and scale. After that, it was just a matter of spinning up a report on LinkedIn ad activity and getting it to the right people on the SDR team. We hadn't busted our silos, but we had certainly made a dent.

WHAT IS AN SDR?

Sales development is a specialized function responsible for outbound prospecting and inbound lead qualification with the goal of generating sales meetings and pipeline. An SDR is a sales development representative. This role is referred to by many names—SDR, BDR, ADR, LDR—and can vary between specialized outbound, inbound, or "allbound" (owning both inbound and outbound for assigned accounts).

Do not use as: a catch-all function. SDRs should not be treated as schedulers, telemarketers, or gophers. People in this role quickly lose their effectiveness in the ABM framework if you're tempted to push them toward doing stuff that's "convenient" for you, but not what they are best at.

If you don't have an ABM team or SDRs working in your organization now, that's totally fine. For earlier-stage companies, marketing campaign managers can play the role of ABM, and sales account executives can play the role of SDRs. This initial collaboration or experiment doesn't have to be in the realm of ABM at all. Here are some examples of small-scale projects you can tackle together.

Set a process goal. Fine-tune one of the ways your departments share information or support each other. It can be as simple as saying, "Any time a salesperson needs X, they should reach out to their defined marketing counterpart to activate Y." This is an easy step to measure as you work toward alignment.

Review an account list together before launching marketing and sales activities. So simple, but so fantastically effective.

Replicate something that worked. If you tried a specific approach in one region and it went well, expand to other regions and track your results.

Gather input from sales on a specific account or set of accounts that have similar attributes. Use this information to create a unique web page with content tailored to the topics those accounts care about. Sales can use this in their outreach efforts.

Review an account plan with a sales rep, if they have one. Listen to what their plans are and identify one way marketing can support them. This is a first step in being sales-focused.

Even having a conversation about a goal you share could count as a small win. What you're doing here is building trust, slowly but surely. That trust will grow quickly if you choose to do things in alignment, see positive results, and celebrate those results together.

We know from our consulting experience with companies large and small that getting a few proof points and some key conversations moving are catalysts for bringing teams together. Before you do any expensive experimentation or role shuffling, before you change processes or find a champion in the C-suite, just *talk* to each other. Find common ground and start collaborating.

Once you've done a few small, collaborative projects, you may feel ready to tackle something more significant. Follow that feeling and build toward an ongoing, productive relationship between the sales and marketing teams. You might not be able to make sweeping departmental changes just yet, but you can still level up your alignment efforts.

In our opinion, this is the perfect time to start dabbling in account-based strategy, especially if your initial efforts to scale your partnership efforts don't get as much traction as you'd like. Why does this work where other sales/marketing unification tactics fall short? Because it distributes the necessary work among tiered experts. Embracing a one-team GTM approach enables the entire sales and marketing group to identify top targets, then divide up the work needed to land those deals among specialists who know exactly how and when to reach out. It's strategic, precise, and yields amazing results quickly enough to generate real excitement.

ABM and SDR: A Match Made in Heaven

For the two of us, learning about and leveraging the sales development representative (SDR) function to bridge the gap between sales and marketing was revolutionary. Practicing account-based motions in partnership with SDRs created an opportunity to multiply our success that may not have been achievable otherwise. It created a one-two punch that helps both teams be more effective. Catalyzing these roles helps everyone across both departments work more efficiently. We all win.

Here's the quick-and-dirty summary of how this collaboration works in practice: In close partnership with the sales team, the ABM team identifies a handful of prime accounts that merit pursuit. This can happen in a few ways:

ABM brings accounts to the table, leading with data for sales to consider prioritizing.

Sales tells ABM they are interested in a specific topic, and the ABM team generates a list of ripe accounts with whom the topic will resonate. (The list is drawn from studying intent data.)

Sales gives ABM a list of accounts that are must-win, regardless of intent data, timing, or other factors.

The SDR team identifies a spike in inbound leads among a specific buying group in an otherwise dormant account.

The SDR team uncovers a relevant corporate initiative shared by a decision-maker via LinkedIn.

In any of these scenarios, the ABMer (how we fondly refer to ABM team members), SDR, and salesperson should be working together to identify the accounts and business units or subsidiaries within the accounts.

Once key people at the accounts have seen bespoke messaging for long enough across online and offline channels to recognize the value add, the SDR team is waiting to reach out to these leads, qualify them, and push them further down the sales funnel. When the sales execs are ready to close the deal, it's easier for them to get into the right conversations with the right people at the top of the funnel, then expedite the process at the middle and bottom of the funnel since the full buying team is already engaged. With this breakdown of duties, everyone is able to execute on their strengths, play their part in warming up the customer, and move together toward the same horizon. This can be done in a highly strategic way at virtually any scale, from one-to-one to one-to-many.

And it works. Spectacularly. We're not the only ones who think so:

A recent benchmarking study from Momentum ITSMA revealed that 72 percent of companies surveyed believe ABM delivers higher ROI than any other type of marketing.[2]

---

2   Leavitt, Rob. "ABM Beyond Revenue: The Other Two R's." Momentum ITSMA. July 19, 2017. https://momentumitsma.com/abm-beyond-revenue-two-rs/.

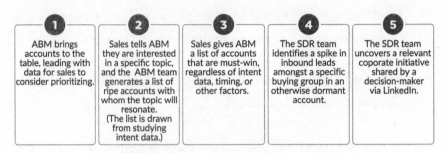

1	2	3	4	5
ABM brings accounts to the table, leading with data for sales to consider prioritizing.	Sales tells ABM they are interested in a specific topic, and the ABM team generates a list of ripe accounts with whom the topic will resonate. (The list is drawn from studying intent data.)	Sales gives ABM a list of accounts that are must-win, regardless of intent data, timing, or other factors.	The SDR team identifies a spike in inbound leads amongst a specific buying group in an otherwise dormant account.	The SDR team uncovers a relevant coporate initiative shared by a decision-maker via LinkedIn.

Sales Development, ABM and Sales can identify accounts together in a multitude of ways, listed above.

After instituting ABM practices, fifty companies surveyed by TOPO saw a 171 percent increase to their average contract value ($195,294 versus $71,941).[3]

And perhaps most significantly, joint Marketo and ReachForce research found that businesses are 67 percent better at closing deals when their sales and marketing teams work together.[4]

To us, this just makes sense. Two teams with a shared goal are going to make more headway on that goal if they join forces. And while marrying *all* of sales to *all* of marketing in one grand gesture might not work, getting a small group of like-minded people to plan and execute a couple of plays together is less daunting and relatively easy to do.

That said, creating a one-team GTM mechanism within your company because it's easy will end in disaster. So will pursuing account-based as a strategy because it's trendy. You need a bigger, more strategic reason to plow ahead. How will this work feed the overall

3   "ABM Alliance Research Shows Payoffs In Retention & Lifetime Value." ABM In Action. February 16, 2017. https://abminaction.com/topics/abm-by-the-numbers/abm-alliance-research-shows-payoffs-in-retention-lifetime-value/.

4   Draper, Alan. "Dynamic Duo: Close More Deals with Sales and Marketing Alignment." Business 2 Community. April 7, 2016. https://www.business2community.com/brandviews/marketo/dynamic-duo-close-deals-sales-marketing-alignment-01505333.

company goals? Why is this a methodology that merits investigation? You may be starting small now—potentially just you and your one ally—but eventually you'll want to scale. If you intend to pitch one-team GTM to the VP or board and ask for their buy-in, you need a solid, logic-backed, data-driven reason why they should support you.

And we'll spend all of the next chapter helping you find that "why."

MINIMUM VIABLE BUY-IN
You and one other person

SCALED BUY-IN
C-level/head of leadership . . . but don't worry about this yet unless it's happening naturally (and quickly!)

MISTAKES TO AVOID
Don't abandon what's working for you. There are plenty of things that sales and marketing do separately and do well apart from each other.

Don't pitch or do a hard sell when you approach your partner on the opposite side of the aisle. Go in ready to learn and listen from your counterpart in sales or marketing.

Don't get discouraged if it doesn't go well the first time. Experiment, iterate, keep trying.

2

Find Your Why

Snowflake is regarded as legendary for scaling at light speed, and what made that speed possible is our highest-level company goals.

Early on, Snowflake defined its mission to mobilize the world's data by building the greatest data and applications platform, and we didn't want to do that at a leisurely pace. We knew that to truly achieve this goal, we needed to grow our company at a rate that kept up with the growth of business and tech overall. So we set our sights on hyper-growth.

Since our IPO, we've nearly tripled our employee head count, with offices in more than thirty countries, and expanded our product offerings to deliver the Data Cloud across industries.[1] And we did it very intentionally by setting truly audacious benchmarks.

---

1   "Snowflake Fast Facts." Snowflake. October 1, 2022. https://www.snowflake.com/wp-content/uploads/2021/05/SnowflakeFastFactsSheet.pdf.

Leadership set six-year company-wide goals to triple our growth every single year of the first three years, then double growth every year of the following three years. As in triple, triple, triple, double, double, double. And we did it.

Most companies struggle to scale that much, especially at that speed. We did it because we linked hyper-growth to our "why."

Envy of growth in scale is a very real force in the market. Company leaders see their competitors gobbling up new business and feel pressured to keep pace. So much of today's growth is supported by tech innovations, it becomes easy to believe that buying the same tech as your rivals could lead to the same growth patterns.

If your organization is a startup, you're probably feeling additional pressure from your VCs. If you are the founder, head of marketing, or head of sales at a small but growing company, your funders will be eager to see evidence of fast, but efficient, growth. That's a hard balance to strike.

Which is how so many of us become bandwagon-hoppers. We figure we'd better adopt any new tech that our peers are adopting and learn how to make it work as quickly as we can. This is how we end up with boatloads of software, dashboards, and subscription plans, plus an endless stream of consultants teaching us how to reframe our mindsets. New tools and frameworks are being created and released at such a clip that if we pause to consider their utility in our own organizations, we risk being left behind.

Hopping on a bandwagon first and sussing out the details later can work occasionally, but it's much more likely to backfire. Which is why we're going to spend this chapter helping you decide if the one-team GTM approach is right for you, and, if so, *why*. We love it ourselves to the point that we live and breathe it every day of our working lives, but that doesn't mean we think it'll be a perfect fit for every company in every industry.

Before you make role changes, invest money, or change strategies, *you must know why one-team GTM is a smart strategic move for your unique organization.*

What Will One-Team GTM Do for You?

To quickly review, one-team GTM is the unified, scaled strategy and execution of an account-based motion across GTM teams. It's the practice of picking a handful of top customers in conjunction with sales, creating bespoke messaging for them, collaborating with SDRs to qualify them, and *then* bookending with a sales executive to drive and close the deal. It can even accelerate that deal, but we'll get into that later in chapter 12.

So given that, what is one-team GTM going to improve within the walls of your organization? When you look at your marketing and sales data right now, where do you see gaps? Where are you lagging? Again, this doesn't have to be a case of "fixing" something that's broken; it can be about improving on current results or augmenting existing strategies. Which customers are you netting that sales would love to clone and land more of?

Here are some common answers that indicate one-team GTM is a fit:

You need to close bigger deals: Just like you expect a more personalized experience when you're buying a home versus buying a latte, your highest-paying customers expect a more robust and bespoke buying experience than your lower-paying ones. (And they are well worth the extra expense.) If your company wants or needs to close high-priced deals, you need the right people, tactics, and tools to approach the buyers for those deals in a savvy and effective way. For many, that way is through an account-based approach. The higher the average selling price and net retention rate, the more likely you are to see efficient unit economics with a spearfishing approach.

It's worth noting that for recurring-revenue businesses, dedicated account-based efforts increase the cost of customer acquisition, which puts a greater burden on the value of each customer. In other words, one-team GTM is a serious investment. But if you already have a high average contract value, you want to increase your average contract value, or absolutely need to land bigger deals with higher-paying customers, an investment in ABM should be worth your while.

You need to prioritize your sales and marketing efforts more effectively: Your target addressable market (TAM) should affect your go-to-market model since it dictates breadth as opposed to depth. The bigger the TAM, the more impersonal you can afford to be. The smaller the TAM, the more you need to roll out focused, customized outreach tactics.

Essentially we're saying that if you take the same approach to engaging one hundred accounts as you do to engaging ten thousand, you'll fail. Try to give too much personal attention to the ten thousand, and your teams will burn out and quit. Approach your top one hundred with a mass-market, templated approach that works just fine for low-priority accounts, and they'll be so insulted they'll never return your calls. The size of your TAM dictates the style of your approach, and different approaches need different people to execute them.

Companies with a smaller, well-defined TAM have to apply surgical precision to their outreach efforts. They are aiming for a handful of prime customers, and those customers only, so every move they make must count. Account-based provides a fantastic level of precision for companies in this position since it encompasses bespoke messaging and targeted outreach.

If you have a list of seventy-five accounts that the sales and marketing groups *must* land or die trying, one-team GTM might be a good fit for you.

You're struggling to effectively engage with buying teams: Selling to a single buyer is completely different from selling to a buying committee. Do IT, a line of business leader, and the CFO all need to say "yes" for the deal to get done? Are there several people who can kill the deal with a single "no"? If so, ABM can efficiently deliver your value proposition to each of these stakeholders in their own language, maximizing the chances that they will support (or at least not block) the sale. How? By giving you multiple people with specialized skills to ensure each committee member is primed to say "yes."

Covering all that ground is complex and challenging. Made even more so by the fact that our sellers are seeing an increasingly large portion of their customers' research completed anonymously (as in, not in coordination with a salesperson). Creating targeted experiences for high-value customers to consume during this anonymous portion of the buying cycle is critical to the larger selling process.

Still not sure if one-team GTM will be a perfect fit or if you can justify the investment? Unsure how to frame that all-important Big Why? We created this diagnostic flowchart to help you consider multiple factors simultaneously and make an informed choice:

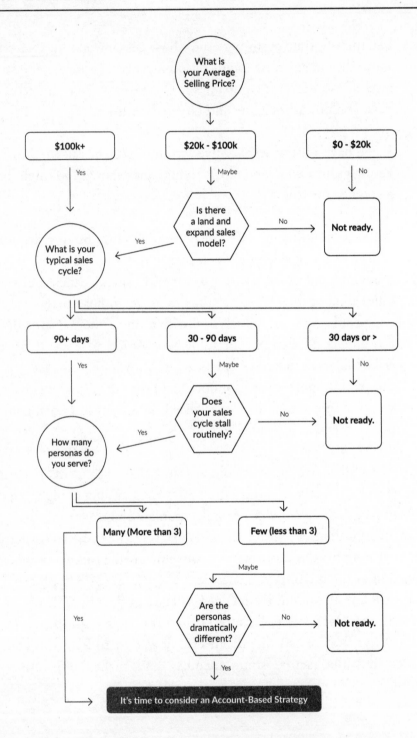

INSIDE THE IGLOO WITH SNOWFLAKE:

Frank Slootman, CEO at Snowflake, on securing entire markets by securing key accounts

Snowflake's visionary CEO has more than twenty-five years of experience as an entrepreneur and executive in the enterprise software industry. Frank served as CEO and president of ServiceNow and president of the Backup Recovery Systems Division at EMC following an acquisition of Data Domain Corporation/Data Domain, Inc., where he served as the CEO and president, leading the company through an IPO to its acquisition by EMC. Frank holds undergraduate and graduate degrees in economics from the Netherlands School of Economics, Erasmus University Rotterdam.

We asked him to speak about the importance of landing the biggest logos in an industry as a business strategy and how doing so has benefited Snowflake's growth.

> When I first arrived at Snowflake, I remember listening to a sales leader going through his forecast, and I don't think I recognized a single name on all the accounts he was targeting. I didn't want us to mindlessly pile on logos, thinking any logo was a good logo. That's not how you win markets. That's not the psychology of markets. When you go into a city or country or a vertical or a sub-vertical, there are accounts there that will dominate the direction of that market by their choices.
>
> For example, hypothetically if you're targeting Minneapolis you might start by trying to secure 3M. It's hard to do, but once you get 3M, everybody in Minneapolis pays attention. If you land Cargill, everybody pays attention. You take three more, you lock them down, you own Minneapolis. You don't even have to work at it anymore; they will fall into your lap.

This happens because people are afraid to make decisions. They're afraid for their job security, and they're afraid of becoming an outlier. So many will watch what industry leaders are doing and then they're going to take a safe position by being a follower. It's called herd mentality, and it works across verticals, cities, regions, and even countries.

This means you need to identify who you must have as accounts for your business. Tier one, tier two, tier three. They're the hardest to penetrate, and there's a reason for that. Otherwise, everybody would do it. And that would be game over. If you do the opposite and go for low resistance, low-hanging fruit, you'll snap up those accounts quickly, but it doesn't help you in markets. You will never win markets that way. You're already losing, and you don't even know it yet.

Prioritizing must-have accounts is not an optional thing. Don't tell yourself, "Oh, I'll get around to it." No, you must do it as soon as you can, because otherwise momentum is against you. The world is always full of momentum. It's either with you or against you; it's never neutral. You need to be very purposeful in managing and driving momentum where you need it to go so your energy isn't wasted and dissipated along the way. If you focus on knocking down those key logos, momentum will be with you. It's immensely powerful.

What If You're *Not* Ready for One-Team GTM?

So, you've just used our handy diagnostic and discovered that your company should hold off on implementing account-based tactics. Your *why* simply hasn't surfaced yet. What now?

Don't abandon all hope of uniting your sales and marketing teams. Here's what you can do instead to keep that momentum going.

Start smaller: Maybe your organization doesn't need the support of a fleet of ABM experts and top-notch SDRs, but there might be *part of your business* that would benefit greatly from this strategy and is described by one or many of the qualifiers listed above. There could be a single working group or project that would love nothing more than to recruit a single marketer and single SDR to help them warm up key prospects. Or perhaps your company sells mainly to individuals and small businesses, but also has an enterprise team; those folks might be overjoyed to experiment with you. There may be a small-scale way to start applying ABM, if you're willing to seek it out.

Keep experimenting: Remember in chapter 1 when we gave you some examples of small collaborative projects to tackle as ways to unite sales and marketing (review an account plan, set a process goal, etc.)? Keep doing those! You can even try a few lean, cheap, two- or three-person account-based plays as experiments. Here are some possibilities:

Retargeting formerly closed lost opportunity accounts

Targeting ads to prospects who are already in active SDR sequences

Direct mail campaign with a call and email follow-up motion

Identify competitive install base and run takeout campaign

Tailored offers for companies receiving funding rounds or showing intent

(We'll show you more plays in more detail in chapter 7, too.) If none of these seem feasible, that's fine, too. Keep taking small steps toward getting your sales and marketing teams into alignment, even if it means doing tiny experiments with one ally and starting a whisper campaign about how fantastic they are. Continue to build bridges by tackling quick collaborations that yield measurable results.

> **Be patient:** As a reader of this book, you're clearly interested in a one-team approach yourself. That probably means that if your current employer isn't fully ready for it, you believe they will be soon. And if not, that you are keeping your eye out for opportunities to engage this practice elsewhere. As someone who believes in the outbound motion inherent to one-team GTM, you'll be primed and ready whenever the opportunity comes along to apply it. And if you keep experimenting, collaborating, and doing whatever you can to unite sales and marketing, you'll have an additional advantage: You'll know how to build bridges and have a clear picture of how much more effective aligned teams can be. Studying account-based principles and the frameworks in this book will benefit any sales and marketing unification work you're doing now and will definitely help you in other roles in the future.

Finding the driving reason for adopting a unified account-based approach is critical, but it won't get you anywhere if people don't embrace it. Key factors that may hold them back? Compensation structures and conflict over attribution. When you're getting people aligned around your why, you must think about how people are paid, recognized, and organized. If sales relies on bonuses that will disappear with an account-based implementation, you'll have a tough time getting them on board. If marketing isn't ready to charge into a workflow without tracking leads and traditional metrics, telling them about the importance of "deal size" will be a waste of breath. Your next steps are going to involve a long, hard look at the way you define "success" inside your organization. How are people being incentivized? What benchmarks are being tracked? How do teams know when they've hit an important goal?

Since this is a complex and delicate set of considerations, we'll spend the whole next chapter talking about attribution, taking credit, and how to recast the work we all do in a more constructive light. And since that work must be driven by shared objectives, we'll help you connect metrics to the reasons you're pursuing one-team GTM in the first place. After all, when you're unsure of how to measure the success of your *why*, you can't make meaningful progress. Instead of forging ahead, you'll stay frozen in place. The topics we cover in the coming chapter will ensure that you can clearly identify what success looks like so you can embrace it, celebrate it, and build upon it.

MINIMUM VIABLE WHY
You are responsible for some portion of GTM in sales or marketing with a large set of accounts, and it is worth your time to align with your cross-functional counterpart(s) to become more effective in prioritized accounts.

SCALED WHY
Your organization needs to go after bigger accounts to hit lofty revenue targets.

MISTAKES TO AVOID
Don't do it because everyone's doing it.

Don't be too general with your why: get specific.

Don't dive in without setting parameters around what success looks like.

Don't get bogged down by how big the work might be, but also don't bite off more than you can chew.

3

Forget Attribution and Focus on Metrics That Matter

Imagine you're working on an assembly line making cars. Everyone contributes their part to the final product, and each car that rolls off the line reflects a win for the entire team. After years of being paid at an hourly rate, the bosses suddenly announce that employees will be compensated based on their percentage of contribution to each car.

You install carburetors in three different car models, and now have to make a case for the importance of your work. Do you measure how much the carburetor contributes to the car's overall weight? Somehow calculate its importance to how the car runs? Figure out how many total parts are in the car, and derive your percentage from that number?

You can probably see where we're headed with this.

Attribution is a huge part of modern work culture, but it can also be a zero-sum game. Especially when you work in marketing, where everything you do contributes to multimedia, multifront campaigns where measuring individual contributor impact is virtually impossible.

The person who created the pitch deck may have influenced a sale closer to the bottom of the funnel, but billboards and online ads could have done some subtle warm-up work long before that.

On top of being tricky to calculate, traditional attribution drives a wedge between sales and marketing. Obsessing over who's pulling their weight or driving results across functions pits people against each other. Especially when you're moving your organization toward a one-team strategy, a dynamic that requires trust and teamwork.

Let's say you're part of an ABM team and you're working directly with a specific sales team. You work with field marketing to launch an event for a prospective client company that gets a C-level person to show up. This individual ends up making the decision to become your customer. The sales team sent the invite directly to the C-level person who showed up at the event, so they want the credit. Your ABM team dreamed up the event based on sales feedback and field marketing planned and executed it, thus giving sales the opportunity to send the invite, so you both also want the credit.

Many companies use carefully calibrated attribution methods to try to circumvent this conflict. They may track first touch, last touch, time decay, or U-shaped patterns in attribution. There are any number of ways to determine who is ultimately responsible for a sale. The problem is that, "Who deserves the credit for this win?" is the wrong question entirely. And these models can't answer it anyway. They can answer much more specific questions like, "Does this type of event better engage net-new prospects than our webinar events?" or "Does this ad drive breadth in a buying committee better than our email nurtures?" But not, "Who should be recognized as the ultimate driver of this deal?"

The *right* question is, "What is the total revenue that we drove for the company together?" That question goes back to the big, over-arching goal that marketing and sales share, a goal that should always be kept in mind. But if you drill down a little deeper, secondary questions include: "What tactics within our process worked well?" and "How do we do more of what worked well, and divest of tactics that didn't work?"

Travis experienced this firsthand when consulting for an early-stage short-term-rental technology startup. The executive team he was working with were well aware that the company had a pipeline problem. There weren't enough qualified deals in the forecast to hit bookings commitments for investors and the board. Sales and marketing were both falling short. As he pulled up an account-based view of the company's funnel (i.e., how target accounts were progressing between stages), he identified that the majority of outbound activities were focused on the smallest accounts. These accounts were converting at a lower rate and at a lower average deal size than the "upmarket" accounts that were getting less attention. SDRs were burning phone calls, and marketing was wasting ad spend going after the wrong segment. Simply flipping the focus of the GTM motion was enough to get the pipeline back into a healthy state.

We believe measurements and metrics are most useful when they prompt self-reflection and help us understand what happened, why, and how to improve on our outcomes in the next go-around. They are far less useful—and accurate—as markers of individual success.

We know that attribution impacts pay, promotions, and job security, so it's not to be taken lightly. But if you want to embrace the one-team motion with both arms, we need to nudge you toward other, more holistic means of measuring success.

Sell for Today, Prep for Tomorrow

While both teams need to keep an eye on their contributions to that overarching revenue goal we've mentioned, there is a key driver to the growth equation: pipeline. We are big fans of focusing on pipeline. As a tool for understanding success over time, pipeline strikes the balance between a leading indicator that provides quick feedback on tactics and a lagging indicator that determines if strategies are paying off.

For most companies, it simply takes too long to understand how your marketing efforts are driving actual revenue. If you wait until you've got data showing which tactics lead directly to closed won deals, you lose speed in making better go-to-market decisions. Note that those of you with more transactional sales cycles (up to ninety days or so) don't need to worry as much about this time delay. What about operating from fast feedback metrics like website visitors or email opens? Focusing on these kinds of leading indicators alone results in optimizing for an outcome that's likely not meaningful. Who cares if you're massively boosting digital engagement if it's with the wrong audience and yielding a trickle of opportunity volume? Pipeline balances these approaches as our "golden metric," the tracks laid down in front of the ever-accelerating revenue train.

We think Snowflake CEO Frank Slootman explained this best in one of his company-wide emails:

"A wise sales manager once told me that a good quarter is not just one where you make the numbers, but also one that sets you up for the next one. Like most enterprise software companies, we cannot both generate the demand and the sales all in the same period. Not even close. Most of the business that comes in has been started a long time ago. . . . Sales campaigns develop over many periods, so while you're out there closing deals you also need to start threads that will close in subsequent periods, if not years."

Any veteran salesperson worth their salt will back Frank up, here. If you only meet your sales numbers for the current quarter and fail to get anything teed up for the coming quarter, you've put yourself in a real bind. Both marketing and sales share the goal of generating revenue, and that means generating revenue in a steady, strategic, ongoing way. It means filling the sales pipeline.

PIPELINE VS. PIPELINE COVERAGE

Pipeline is defined as the total number of potential deals that have been qualified as viable selling opportunities by an AE, but have not yet been closed.

Pipeline coverage is a ratio used by the sales team to measure how much revenue is covered by the deals sitting in the pipeline compared to the new revenue target they need to hit. This is calculated by dividing the pipeline revenue over a certain period by the target new revenue for the same period.

At Snowflake, our pipeline-filling efforts are prescriptive, calculating the pipeline coverage required for future quarters and then following up with the appropriate actions to help us *reach* that coverage goal.

In order to do this, we calculate:

The average sales win rate, which is the percentage of closed won deals out of total deals worked during the period

The average sales price (ASP), which is the average dollar value of closed won deals. (This is also known as ACV, which means annual contract value)

The sales cycle time, which is the average number of days from qualifying an opportunity to winning it

We then apply these assumptions to the total dollars we need to win in a given period.

FORMULA: Closed Won Target / Average Win Rate / Average Sales Price

Let's make this a bit more tangible. Assume your board has defined a target of $10M in closed won dollars in Q4 and you have a win rate of 25 percent and ASP of $100k. This means you need at least $40M in pipeline (roughly four hundred opportunities) set to close in Q4 in order to have enough buffer to hit your goal. Simple enough—that is your basic pipeline coverage target.

Here's an example of what that looks like when you overlay your actual pipeline coverage with your target pipeline coverage:

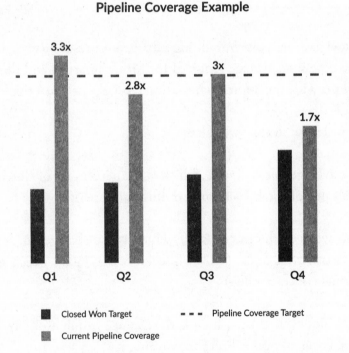

This GTM team could see at a glance that Q2 could use some strengthening while Q4 should be the major focus of pipeline-generating efforts.

To make this actionable, you also need to understand *when* you should be creating these opportunities. This is where we think many organizations fall short. If your average sales cycle is one hundred days, then a portion of those four hundred opportunities will need to be created in advance of Q4 in order to have enough time to mature and close in that period. You can use that time delay to build a "pipeline creation schedule" that tells your GTM teams exactly how much pipeline should be produced at any point throughout the fiscal year. For example, pipeline created in January will likely close about one hundred days later in the April/May time frame.

Travis has seen this issue crop up time and again when working specifically with sales organizations who have a demand problem. They tend to correctly identify that more meetings are needed to drive more opportunities, but they habitually recognize this problem too late. Because of the typical time delay, you can't start booking meetings today that will save your pipeline this month or this quarter (with the exception of extremely high velocity businesses with very short sales cycles). Understanding that today's meetings are next quarter's (or next year's) deals completely shifts the conversation for sales leaders and changes what they ask of their demand-generating counterparts in sales development and marketing.

We recommend building on those basics to set more accurate goals by considering the following:

Planning for Pipeline Decay: Sales teams tend to shift attention at the end of the quarter from closing new deals to cleaning up their forecast numbers for the next quarter. Pipeline will push out, contract, and vanish altogether as deals get updated. You can build this into your pipeline coverage target to de-risk the plan. Ten percent is a reasonable buffer to start with. You can get more exact by looking back at previous quarters and comparing the pipeline amount ninety days before the quarter compared to the pipeline amount on day one of the quarter. This tells you the typical pipeline "falloff" for your business.

Adjusting Win Rate by Opportunity Stage: Opportunities in later stages generally have a higher probability of closing than earlier stage opportunities. You can use this to fine-tune near-term pipeline coverage goals versus coverage for periods farther out in the future. You can fine-tune this by weighting the value of pipeline depending on the stage of the opportunity. For example, applying a 10 percent weight to pipeline in the first stage of your sales process.

Localizing Goals: If your business operates in multiple countries or maintains multiple sales segments, you may have radically different pipeline assumptions in different parts of the company. You can waterfall the global pipeline coverage and creation goals down to those groups to provide more surgical targets.

At Snowflake, we leverage a machine learning model built within the Snowflake product to precisely predict our pipeline coverage, taking into account all of the above. This single view for sales and marketing has become a unifying element for how we plan activities together throughout the year, just like we are recommending you to do as well. We will show you how to build this using Snowflake yourself in the final chapter, and share insights from the data scientist responsible for it.

Bottom line, you need to rally your marketing, SDR, and sales teams around the single, overarching goal of pipeline coverage. Only then can you meaningfully measure the strategies and tactics deployed by each team.

Here's what that looks like inside Snowflake.

INSIDE THE IGLOO WITH SNOWFLAKE:

Mark Fleming, SVP of Americas Enterprise at Snowflake, on the critical importance of pipeline coverage

An enterprise sales leader with twenty-one years of experience at enterprise technology organizations, Mark has gone from leading sales teams at companies such as Oracle, Apple, and EMC to building early stage go-to-market teams at Platfora (acquired by Workday) and prior to Snowflake, Pure Storage. Mark's seen the sales cycle from many perspectives and counts himself fortunate to have joined two companies during the energizing pre-IPO stage, first at Pure Storage and most recently at Snowflake. When he's not cheering on his children at various school and sporting endeavors, he can be found cheering for his favorite Boston-based sports teams and balancing work with fitness to stay sane.

We asked him to speak about the strategic importance of pipeline coverage as a one-team metric, and pipeline knowledge as a tool for sales forecasting.

We have three hundred sellers across the United States in my department, which is the enterprise go to market, and we represent a little bit over a billion dollars in revenue for Snowflake's business, so pretty material. A big part of what we do is try to forecast as accurately as we can how much revenue our group will be making. We try to be within a 3 to 5 percent variance on the call from week one, month one of each quarter. Being able to call that number early on has a lot to do with the backward look and the forward look.

So historically, sales teams work in the 30-60-90-day mindset: You close a quarter, you wake up, it's day one, and you say to yourself, "Oh no, we gotta start bringing in some business." As you get into frontline, second-line, third-line, and beyond

CRO level, you really have to have teams thinking about the out quarters. That's really what I think we've done a great job of doing here. And the synergy and partnership that we have with the SDR team and the ABM team is really around that forward-looking pipeline, which is the trailing indicator of the work that's happening.

At a lot of companies, the sales revenue goal would be somewhat of an arbitrary number . . . or you'd look at the quota, you look at your goal, and you'd land somewhere around that. At Snowflake, we've done a really good job, particularly over the last year, I think we've really dug in to setting that number through pipeline review, the backward-looking pipeline.

To make sure our forecasts are as accurate as possible, we make sure that pipeline hygiene is as dialed in as it can be. We don't have a bunch of extra placeholders or multimillion-dollar deals that are going to skew our numbers. So by the time we arrive at our month-two inspection point, all my RVPs have taken at least a first or a second pass at the quarter pipeline. This keeps us from having what I call "a feel-good funnel," where everybody feels like, "Oh, we've definitely got 4X coverage." But when you actually poke at it, you see those deals aren't real, or too many of them are placeholders.

I can call up one of my RVPs and say, "You're gonna miss your number in Q4." And they'll say, "It's Q1, how do you know that?" And the answer is pipeline inspection. Either your team's not showing their work, or we don't have enough coverage. So let's go build a plan. And this isn't to catch people out. It's more about saying, "You're going to crash into the rocks. We have all the time in the world, so let's course correct now before that happens."

I've worked at big 60,000+ person organizations and really small ones where I was the first hire on a sales team. And at all of them, there was always a fight over attribution. Like, "this came from the Insight team," "This came from the channel team," or "This box wasn't checked." I don't have time for any of that noise. I personally don't care about the attribution. Because at the end of the day, if we're adding pipeline, that's what we care about. Our job is to drive revenue for Snowflake. Our job is to build pipeline so we have accurate coverage. So we don't wake up in Month One or Q1 and say, "We're gonna miss our number," because that's just not acceptable, particularly when you're a publicly traded company.

Zooming in on Pipeline: An Account Funnel

We've established that pipeline is the most important outcome, but now we want to give you a guide to the metrics that matter in generating that pipeline. You need to track the leading indicators of your account-based efforts with an account-based funnel, rather than a lead funnel.

At Snowflake, we divide our account funnel into six stages:

Target Accounts are accounts receiving any ABM treatment at all. (This is our largest pool, at the top of the funnel.)

Engaged Accounts have a high likelihood of becoming sales qualified opportunities based on engagement. We also refer to these as MQA's or Marketing Qualified Accounts.

Working Accounts have at least one logged SDR/AE activity in the past ninety days.

Meeting Accounts have had at least one meeting completed with the sales team.

Opportunity Accounts have at least one open opportunity.

Won Accounts have at least one closed won opportunity.

What about all the acronyms? Don't you need SAOs, SQLs, and SALs to have a true funnel? We find that our favorite acronyms in sales and marketing land add little value while continuously confusing our partners in the business. That's why we are fans of strikingly clear funnel stage names like "Opportunity Accounts."

For us, pipeline is generated at the point when accounts move from Meeting Accounts to Opportunity Accounts. Our job is to move them. But we also need to be moving other account types through the funnel simultaneously so there are enough accounts at each level that are all moving toward becoming Won Accounts that we can then renew and expand.

As we do the work of moving accounts to new levels, we use inspection metrics to understand how well our tactics are working. Inspection metrics are questions we ask and performance KPIs we track that help us see where our processes might be breaking down. We examine them between funnel stages, but track them at all times.

For strategic reasons, the ABM team uses different tactics and messaging for each of these six account funnel stages; a Working Account is going to get different treatment from us (invites to live events, custom emails from SDRs) than a Target Account (customized landing pages, retargeted ads). So to determine measurements that matter and continually improve the work we're doing, we need to use different inspection metrics for each stage.

How does the account funnel work? Let's say your team is currently focused on getting more Target Accounts to become Engaged Accounts. That means you need to know how to increase conversion between those levels, and metrics that reveal which tactics are working best. At Snowflake we ask ourselves, "How effective are our outward tactics at creating inward engagement from our prospects?" At Snowflake we track a few inspection metrics to answer this specific question:

Account Propensity: How likely is this account to respond positively to sales outreach and take a meeting based on technographic and firmographic data that closely mirrors past companies that took the desired action? At Snowflake, we represent this "fit" with a machine learning score, but it can also be represented by other trackable metrics that do not require data science.

Minimum Viable Approach: Identify a list of customers that renew and expand at the highest rates and pinpoint common characteristics like industry, company size, existing tech stack, etc.

Scaled Approach: Purchase a platform with built-in account scoring or build your own account propensity model on a data platform like Snowflake (details covered in chapter 7).

Intent (First Party): How likely is this account to further engage with your marketing and sales efforts based on the behavior they are exhibiting on your own web properties? At Snowflake, we break this down into anonymous and known engagement. If an account has a high volume of web traffic to your site that is identified through a de-anonymization tool, this would be anonymous intent. Once individuals in the account have provided their contact information for an asset or event or responded to a piece of direct mail, we consider this known engagement. We can then create a threshold of cumulative engagement at the account level to determine first-party intent.

Minimum Viable Approach: Track campaign responders grouped at the account level to monitor first-party engagement with your content at that account. Identify a threshold for when you consider an account "engaged."

Scaled Approach: Purchase a platform with built-in predictive models or build your own predictive model that identifies when accounts reach meaningful engagement thresholds.

Intent (Third Party): Does this account have an abnormal increase in behavior signals *outside* your company's properties that indicate a buying cycle is approaching? Signals can vary from a surge in online research about your solution or the specific problem that your solution solves to job postings that list skills needed that are related to your product. You can track a variety of signals relevant to your business with stand-alone third-party intent data providers, a platform with intent capabilities built in, or a combination of both depending on what signals you need.

Minimum Viable Approach: Set up a notification on LinkedIn for when your ideal accounts post job descriptions or when a current customer moves companies. You can use both of these as signals for intent for little to no cost. If you have more budget, subscribe to an intent data source that has the minimum data signals you need to get started.

Scaled Approach: Subscribe to an intent data source(s) that includes a variety of signals including web traffic, content consumption, job postings, social signals, etc.

If we are struggling to move accounts from Target to Engaged, we can dig into the activities related to account propensity (like how we're determining which accounts fit our ideal profile) and intent (like which search terms they're using and how often) and make adjustments to those. Inspection metrics are like diagnostics: They enable us to link our success (or lack of success) directly back to activities and strategies so we can do more of what's working and less of what's not.

The chart below shows an overview of all six stages and how we think about moving accounts from one level to the next. The questions called out in the thought-bubbles are designed to drive improvement in our processes, and the metrics on the far right help us diagnose problems, track performance, and find leaks in our engine.

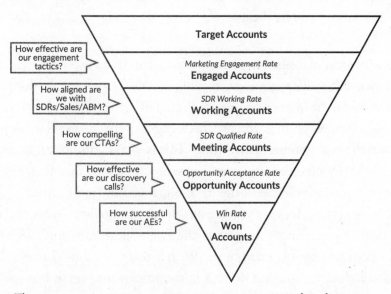

There are many ways to measure success across account-based programs.
Look for inspection metrics for early indicators of success or opportunity.

The account funnel becomes a lens into how your agreed-upon accounts are progressing toward your end goals of building pipeline, then generating revenue. But the inspection metrics we've noted are the true hidden secrets to scalable success. They help you embed the behavior of monitoring your results and using what you've learned to improve future performance. Tracking these metrics helps you build better systems, which is far more valuable than just tinkering with your results. In his book *Atomic Habits*, James Clear explains this beautifully at a personal level, saying:

> We think we need to change our results, but the results are not the problem. What we really need to change are the systems that cause those results. When you solve problems at the results level, you only solve them temporarily. In order to improve for good, you need to solve problems at the systems level. Fix the inputs and the outputs will fix themselves.[1]

In the context of unified marketing efforts, this means *monitoring activity and results while processes are running*, as well as after they're done. In other words, the inspection metrics that sit in between the levels in your account funnel can function as "check engine lights": They'll show you how well your systems are running. This is vitally important, because far too many organizations are unsure how to gauge the efficiency of their systems, which means they're also unsure how to improve.

For example, let's say you create relevant campaigns to touch 100 percent of your Target Accounts, the largest and most undifferentiated pool of possible customers. With a team of aligned marketers and salespeople, you can do this fairly quickly and track how all of

---

1   Clear, James. 2018. *Atomic Habits: Tiny Changes, Remarkable Results : An Easy & Proven Way to Build Good Habits & Break Bad Ones*. New York: Avery, 25.

those accounts respond. But you haven't used any selection criteria before creating the campaigns, and that will backfire in short order.

When you need to reach out to Engaged and Working Accounts, you won't have a clear idea of how your best-performing emails are written, or what they've done to garner high open rates. You won't know how to create CTAs for your digital assets to garner the maximum number of clicks. Because you blanketed everyone with outreach, you have no criteria or data to compare against. How will you optimize future efforts so they lead to engagement?

Working backward even further, if you don't know which factors affect an account's propensity to buy, how will you select the ones that are actually ready to engage? Building a strategic system for selecting accounts and engaging accounts is critical to setting up SDRs and sales for success.

To explore the importance of inspection metrics in even more depth, let's jump a little further down the funnel: Meeting Accounts have had at least one meeting with an AE completed, so they're now getting attention from SDRs in the form of emails and discovery calls. So to generate useful metrics, we ask ourselves the question, "How effective are our discovery calls?" The measurements we use to answer that question are number of meetings per account, meeting hold rate, and number of touches. If those numbers are lower this quarter than they were the previous quarter, then we step back up the funnel to make sure our Working Account system is running smoothly. Did we add an adequate number of contacts to our touch sequence? Did we move contacts from Engaged to Working too quickly? If so, we may increase the engagement threshold that accounts need to hit before being touched by an SDR.

Even the best, most efficient marketing and sales operations run into these sorts of snags. The behavior that separates good from great is taking the time to find the breaks in the system and fix them from the inside out.

As long as the work that marketing and sales, ABMers and SDRs, are all doing moves our accounts from one level to the next, we are gradually filling our pipeline. We can constantly compare that progress against the pipeline-creation schedule we defined earlier. We can zoom in to the team level and see where our progress is lacking. We can also zoom out to the company level and see how close we are to achieving our collective goal.

We hope our own framework for determining metrics is useful to you, but we know that depending on your company size, industry, and resources you may just need to create your own. Doing that begins with thinking about what "success" means in some new— and highly measurable—ways.

Reframing Success

Again, bear in mind that the *ultimate* measure of your success is, "How much total revenue sales and marketing drove for the company," with pipeline coverage serving as the best leading indicator. All other success metrics should ladder back up toward that shared goal in some meaningful way. But teams and departments need to examine their successes on a smaller scale, too, in order to see what's working and refine their tactics.

Aligning on metrics and KPIs at the departmental level can be tricky, but it's a critical component of honing your one-team, account-based work. We suggest deciding which metrics to track based on two overarching themes:

COLLABORATION: Since you're always thinking about busting silos in the back of your mind, it's helpful to assign KPIs to your ongoing collaborative efforts. Here are some examples.

How often are people from sales groups and marketing groups meeting with each other? Such a simple thing to track, but it so clearly shows that communication and cooperative work are happening. Most-engaged reps with ABM should be talking at least once, if not several times per week. Less-engaged would be monthly at a minimum. Having this range of engagement and meetings is not only OK, but necessary to balance workloads in a scaled team.

Are your marketing and SDR teams being invited to quarterly business reviews (QBR) with sales? These meetings are where performance is evaluated and upcoming goals are set. Being asked to attend—or even better, participate—is a signal that your ideas and work have been recognized. At Snowflake, the ABM group, SDRs, and field marketing are all presenting together at QBRs, which is a multilevel signal that we're well aligned.

Are your upcoming quarter initiatives driven by the needs of sales, or have they been created in a void? Through regular conversation and alignment, we want to make sure that whatever our North Stars are for the upcoming quarters directly align to how the sales team plans to go to market.

How many accounts have an account plan? Having a potential customer's info in your database is a start . . . but unless there's a plan to approach them, they're essentially dormant. Tracking the number of accounts with plans in place signals value and lets you know how much new work is coming down the pike.

How many meetings are coming out of ABM-targeted accounts? Focusing on the number of SDR meetings coming out of ABM accounts allows you to both see clear alignment between sales and ABM and to ensure SDR outreach is as effective as possible.

That final example is one that we at Snowflake puzzled out through trial and error. Our account executives (AEs) were accustomed to choosing a list of accounts for an SDR to call into, but those accounts were different from the ones they were prioritizing with the ABM team. So the SDRs and ABMers were being sent in multiple directions at once. Red flag for our goal of aligned execution.

We knew that SDRs were four times more likely to book a meeting when aligned with ABM, so we looked at why we were running in different directions. We found that sales was treating them as two different motions. Naturally, we wanted to encourage the teams to align on one account list between AEs, SDRs, and ABM. We needed a form of measurement to help us know we'd been successful in aligning those teams. If the current situation led to few SDR-booked meetings coming from *accounts also targeted by ABM*, then that number increasing over time would indicate that SDRs and ABM were targeting the same accounts (can't book a meeting in an ABM account if it isn't targeted by ABM!) and that we were aligned.

In being aligned, we all became more effective and efficient. Which leads us to the next theme among useful metrics:

EFFICIENCY: Is what you're doing working? Is it working quickly and affordably? Are people supporting each other effectively? If you are aligned to a common goal, it is in everybody's best interest to get to that goal faster with less effort. Nobody wants to work harder and get there slower. This should be something that everyone can rally behind.

Time to first campaign responder: How long does it take from the time you start targeting an account to the time they first respond?

Number of calls required to first meeting: With aligned efforts among AEs, ABM, and SDRs, are you getting meetings faster and more easily?

Deal acceleration: Is the time-to-close faster than without collaborative efforts?

Metrics aren't just about measuring what's working, they're also about understanding what's failing. Everyone interested in adopting the one-team GTM strategy should become familiar with the check engine lights for its outcomes and processes.

Measuring Waste and Warning Signals

The entire design of an account-based strategy centers on efficiency. It is meant to get the most possible impact out of every action taken and every conversation held. That means if there is wasted time or effort, someone somewhere is focusing on the wrong goals. Someone is confused over which metrics they should be tracking.

Hillary uses this story from her own life to underline this point.

During college, she rowed crew, spending most mornings in a racing shell on the shores of Mission Bay in San Diego as the sun was rising. There are two seasons for crew: long distance in the fall, and sprint in the spring. Winter break separated those two seasons, so Hillary and her teammates had forty-two days off before making the shift. Her coach told the team those forty-two days would determine their success in sprint season. If they collectively chose to work out, eat healthy, and stay in fighting form, then sprint season would go well. If not, by the time the team got back to campus it would be too late. And because the coach wanted the entire team to never, ever forget the importance of their choices during that forty-two day vacation from rowing, he had them call out "forty-two!" whenever they broke from a huddle. That was their point of collective focus.

Most importantly, as the ultimate team sport, if one of the eight crew members hyper-focused on the goal and the seven others didn't, the results would not reflect the effort. All team members had to be charging toward the goal in synchrony to realize the desired outcome.

To shift back to the business world, we believe that having teams train their eyes solely on a number (say, $100,000 pipeline) is marginally helpful . . . but to improve action and accomplish goals, a better mantra would be "SDRs touch every Engaged Account." Why? Because when they touch every account, the pipeline gets filled. And "SDRs touch every Engaged Account" gives people an activity that they can describe and measure, a concrete metric that helps them see clearly if they've been successful or not.

Every team needs their "forty-two!" If your team doesn't know what they're supposed to be rallying around, they'll fly off in a million different directions. And then you get waste, miscommunication, and problems.

We recommend keeping an eye out for these red flags:

Volume Exceeds Quality: If you or your team are fighting bandwidth constraints yet lack measurable results, the value of the approach is getting lost in scale. Step back, re-prioritize your efforts and accounts, and narrow your focus to the activities that have proven to have the largest impact from your prior data.

People are consistently saying, "I didn't know I was supposed to do that." Miscommunication is a death knell, especially when you're working toward a unified sales-marketing power team. If people are unsure of their duties, pinpoint the breakdown in understanding and create clarity ASAP.

Sales and SDRs are consistently saying, "I didn't have time to prioritize these accounts." This is the opposite of efficiency. All

of the mechanisms within one-team GTM are meant to stream-
line work and workloads, so if people are running out of time
to complete their work, something's broken. A priority realign-
ment may be in order.

Off-message content is being used. If ABMers or SDRs are
using the wrong message or sending outdated content, this is
another sign that communication is on the fritz. How is messaging flowing to the people distributing it? Is someone missing
from that chain of communication?

You notice a marked lack of activities. If someone on your
team just isn't doing their work, it can be driven by a number of causes. It might be misunderstanding of roles and duties;
breakdown in communication with sales, marketing, or both;
asking the wrong questions; or just plain failing to collaborate.
Regardless, if someone fails to hit any of their goals, that's a signal that something is badly amiss.

One final note: Plenty of companies invest in prospecting tech without knowing how to run it. Others may hire entire teams of ABM
experts without understanding the mechanism or identifying how it
might support their business model. We believe the biggest warning
signal of all is diving into the account-based world without setting
clear goals around how it will move your company forward. We
dedicated all of chapter 2 to this idea: the undeniable importance of
finding your *why*.

When does attribution make sense?

Now here's a plot twist for you: We don't actually believe that all
attribution is evil and useless.

In our opinion attribution is for comparing tactics, not measuring your strategy. And it shouldn't be attached to people and their

individual performance, but instead associated with specific plays and campaigns.

This will make more sense with an example. Let's say Hillary wants to know which campaigns are doing the best job of grabbing attention from people who have never heard of Snowflake. The company uses first-touch attribution—tracking which marketing activity the person engaged with before offering up their personal information for the first time—and Hillary can see which efforts led to the largest number of responses. If LinkedIn Messaging out-performed webinars in getting first-time responders to click or sign up to get more information, that's incredibly helpful to her. If she wants to build a new campaign around brand awareness, she can replicate what's already worked. First-touch attribution is a tool she can use.

On the other hand, Travis may want to know which campaigns are best at building credibility with buyers who are actively evaluating solutions. In this case, he could use last-touch attribution—tracking which marketing activity the person engaged with immediately before an opportunity was qualified—to understand which campaigns are best at teeing up a prospect for a qualifying conversation with the SDR team.

Abandoning attribution as a means of "staking claims" to customer actions or overall wins doesn't necessitate eliminating attribution altogether. Tracking touch points and understanding how they impact customer actions is still extremely valuable. You just need a different way to view and use the same data. Focus on what you want to know, and use attribution to unlock that insight.

Another aspect of that ongoing refinement process is assessing when to stop certain activities or abandon tactics that just aren't working right.

What Matters Most? Pipeline.

Plenty of experts will tell you to "measure what matters most." In the case of sales and marketing, what matters most is quite simple: it's total pipeline growth. It's finding deals. It's overall revenue generation. If you're measuring and rewarding people using metrics that don't connect back to the pipeline, it's time to reevaluate.

Here's a little proof that we practice what we preach. As we were reviewing our past decks while writing this book, we came across this slide:

PURPOSE

ONE CONSISTENT MESSAGE
ONE SET OF ACCOUNTS TO ACHIEVE
ONE GOAL ... Q4 PIPELINE

Making pipeline-building the action focus unites teams, keeps efficiency top-of-mind, prepares everyone for future success, and helps you focus on metrics that matter. It really is the best way to motivate a united sales and marketing team.

We honestly believe if you're using attribution models to allocate bonuses and compensation, you may be doing more harm than good. When it comes to salaries, a simple reframe can help: salespeople are paid on commission, which is the closing of the pipeline, so they're effectively compensated on pipeline contributions already. SDRs are usually paid on quota for the number of sales meetings they book, which are also linked to pipeline. Marketing is trickier because variable compensation is typically structured by a loose bonus incentive based on creating and executing marketing programs. That approach can work, but we recommend getting specific on pipeline-relevant outcomes. At Snowflake, our ABMers and marketers define those outcomes at the start of each quarter: quantifiable goals tied directly to the pipeline coverage goals that have been articulated with sales. This drives their variable compensation in a make-or-miss fashion in alignment with the business.

Bonuses also need to be recast, but it simply isn't realistic for a 500-person marketing team to all have the entirety of their bonuses determined by one line item: total contribution to pipeline. Instead it should be measured on progress indicators toward that common goal of pipeline.

Each company will need to determine those indicators independently, but at Snowflake we subscribe to an effort we call "What Matters," similar to OKRs (objectives and key results). At the beginning of each quarter, the CMO identifies three or four top priorities for the business. Building and exceeding pipeline is always one of them, but landmark company events and third-party events are often others, as well as major product releases. Each of the CMO's direct reports then take their "What Matters" list and create a version of their own that details three or four outcomes they will drive that ladder up to the overall priorities. That process cascades down the org chart so the entire marketing organization has set outcomes they will drive that continue to push the company forward at hyper-growth rates.

An example of this would be our flagship customer event, Snowflake Summit. The CMO might note a priority of X percent growth over the previous year's attendance. The head of demand gen would then commit to driving registrants, the product marketing team would commit to a designated number of sessions, and the PR team would commit to a certain number of media activities, etc. The event is expected to drive a massive amount of pipeline for the business, each group that participates is measured against its own goals, and if they exceed those goals they're rewarded with bonuses.

It's much harder to bust silos when people are rewarded for claiming their specific role in a group effort. (Remember: No one at the car factory wants to be compensated for their percentage contribution to each car.) Pull yourself out of the attribution quagmire, and come join us on solid ground where we focus on how sales and marketing build and fill the pipeline. Yes—this can mean tying marketing bonuses to pipeline outcomes for the company.

Once you've done that, you've laid most of the groundwork for your one-team account-based approach. Keep reading to find out how to start activating the work!

MINIMUM VIABLE METRIC

Whatever you've chosen as your why, know the single metric that shows you're successful at advancing toward it.

SCALED METRICS

Understand the KPIs working backward from that why, including check engine lights. This allows you to scale, enabling you to repeat successful processes across more people.

MISTAKES TO AVOID

Don't try to measure something just because someone else is measuring it at another company.

Don't try to measure too many things. If everything's important, nothing's important.

Don't over-rotate on proving the value of your contribution to the larger picture.

PART 2

WHO AND WHAT

4

Segment the Market

In part 1, we explained why busting silos and marrying sales and marketing is the best possible way to build a GTM motion. Now, in part 2, we'll explore understanding and finding ideal accounts and crafting messages that will be impossible for them to ignore.

Diving into the nitty-gritty of activating your one-team GTM practice is definitely exciting. You've found your allies, done some initial silo-busting, gotten a few key folks aligned, decided how to measure your progress, and now everyone is just itching to sketch out their first plays.

But before you start drafting or sending any emails, we need you to pause. Before you customize landing pages or reach out to *anyone*, you've got to get a clear picture of which accounts you want to target.

And also which ones you *don't* want to target.

Here's a quick story to explain that last point. While we were in the process of writing this book, the two of us happened to run a webinar that drew about five hundred virtual attendees. The purpose of the event was lead generation, and we were happy with the number of people who showed up. Many marketing teams would stop at that number, look over at their sales team, and ask, "Where are you at with follow-up on our five hundred webinar leads?"

We decided to have some fun and dig into the data of those five hundred individuals, knowing exactly what we would find. Naturally, we found that dozens of attendees were our own coworkers at Snowflake checking out what we put together, another bunch worked for our main competitors possibly doing some competitive research, a handful appeared to be students who were sharpening their Data Cloud knowledge, and yet more were individuals already engaged with sales on active opportunities. We would not call any of those "real leads," and you shouldn't either. Yet we've seen *so* many companies get caught in this lead trap because they have not established their TAM or segmented their database. You cannot define what marketing noise you should rightfully ignore until you've defined exactly what companies you want to sell to.

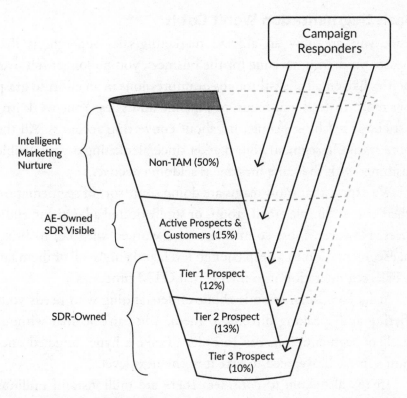

Percentages are for demonstration purposes only. It's critical to categorize the types of accounts that inbound leads belong to. For example, inbound leads from active customer accounts could go directly to the Account Executive with a notification sent to the SDR.

If you don't bother to segment your market, you invest in the wrong places.

And while it takes time to do proper segmentation, this is a "go slow now to go fast later" proposition. Making sure you are speaking to and reaching your target audience right now will help you convert those people in droves farther down the line.

Basic Segmentation Won't Cut It

Since you are now an aligned marketing/sales supergroup that focuses on driving revenue for the business, you no longer fret over metrics like email click-throughs or impressions in an effort to grasp for credit. Instead you focus on pipeline and sales. Your work isn't just about reaching people, it's about converting accounts. All the more reason to segment your market since blanketing every possible customer with the same message is seldom effective.

We expect that most teams are doing some sort of segmentation whether it be simple email groups or sophisticated advertising audiences. However, most companies we've worked with fail to bring that segmentation to a deep enough level, and almost all of them fail to bake segmentation into their actual GTM processes.

At its core, marketing is about understanding who needs your offering and speaking directly to them. You can't do that without excellent segmentation. But in order to take a hyper-targeted one-team approach, we need to take it to the next level.

There's also scale to consider. There are millions and millions of businesses in the world, and you can only sell to a small subset of them. (Especially if you want to sell *successfully*.) You have finite people, budget, and time, all of which must be allotted strategically to generate the maximum amount of revenue for your efforts. When you segment the market, you can concentrate your efforts and creativity mindfully. As the two of us like to say, *ABM is all about accounts, but not all accounts deserve ABM*. Picking and choosing which accounts to target is a critically important part of the motion.

Finally, account-based approaches are grounded in customization. Every piece of content you create and email your team sends is likely to have personal touches. Each account is treated differently, with bespoke messaging and tailor-made strategies. So if you're truly embracing the account-based way, you simply cannot sell to everyone.

A quick note on how the rest of this chapter will work: We wanted to include every element of the segmentation process, but realize some of you may have tackled portions of that work already. If you're a prelaunch startup, you'll need to read everything, including the next section on calculating target addressable market (TAM). But if you're hyper-growth and already know your TAM, you can consider flipping ahead. And if you've already got the building blocks of an account-based practice in place, the section on "dividing the work by group and capacity" is where you may want to start. We leave it to you to decide.

Regardless, though, we believe that focus is your best friend at every stage of your company's growth. And no matter where you are right now, segmenting your market will help you become more successful. So let's talk about how to do it.

Start with Your TAM

How do you determine how many accounts your company should target? How do you decide which companies merit account-based outreach?

We recommend starting with the Target Addressable Market (TAM), the group of specific companies that you believe are a good fit for your product or service, across firmographic, technographic, and other descriptive dimensions. While it's the same acronym, this is different than the Total Addressable Market. We're talking about the specific list of accounts you want to target as opposed to the total value of the market that your business is operating in. Your TAM will give you an incredible sense of focus and define guardrails so you don't attempt to market to everyone. You can begin the process of winnowing down to usable segments by examining your TAM.

TAM CALCULATION CHEAT SHEET

You may already know your TAM, but in case you haven't fully defined it yet, here are our tips. Defining TAM for your company means doing some research about past, current, and ideal customers. Ask questions like:

What are the common features of companies that have a problem you can solve?

What products are those companies using that are complementary with or competitive to your solution?

If you have customers now, what industries have you historically sold to?

Where are your current customers located?

Where are the companies you'd like to sell to located?

How big are those companies?

Make some lists or spreadsheets to capture all of this information, and do any initial winnowing down that you can. For example, if you've historically sold into large real estate operators, but churn has been consistently high among those customers, consider removing that segment from your list.

If you already have access to an internal database of businesses, use it to filter by industry, company size, and location. Keep adding filters to narrow in on your TAM, but try not to add so many that your market opportunities become too small.

With that large pool of possible customers in hand, you can start dividing them into groups and deciding how to address each group strategically.

How to segment the market by labels now that you have TAM

Now you're ready to divide your entire pool of possible customers into groups. The segmenting begins in earnest now! Doing this typically involves augmenting whatever information you've got in your in-house database by drawing on some third-party vendors. You may already have basic or complex segments, but perhaps they need to be revisited with a fresh, account-based eye.

In order to enrich your account information, you will need data intelligence services if you don't already have them. In addition to basics like company name, location, and industry, these services will provide important identifiers like annual revenue, company size, technographic data, growth figures, key contact names and information, and other critical data that you need to segment effectively. Once this information is entered into your own database, you've got a much more robust resource to draw from. The multitude of identifiers that you choose will enable you to slice and dice your segments beyond basic industries and company sizes. Looking at technographic data and firmographic data, for example, can help you identify which companies are likely struggling with problems you can solve. Here's an example:

Let's say you work at a healthcare technology SAAS company with one thousand employees that is ready to expand beyond the single product you launched with. You have researched your new buying personas for your billing product and know who your buying group includes and what technology you are displacing, as well as which size companies are large enough to feel the pain your product solves. You already know that your target industry is healthcare and that your ideal companies have more than five hundred employees. But by using your newly enriched database, you might create more robust customer segments like:

Hospital systems with more than four locations and five hundred administrative employees

Commonality: Disparate ER locations with disconnected billing

Clinic groups with more than six locations that have legacy billing software

Commonality: Collaboration features that will save $500,000 a year in missed billing opportunities

Healthcare providers in a specific state that rolled out new compliance regulations for billing practices

Commonality: Need to migrate technologies to maintain compliance under new regulations

With a few initial segments created, your next step is to start thinking about how your marketing and sales teams will activate them. Which ones will be contacted first, and why? Which ones need lots of customization and individual attention, and which can get more general treatment? We will cover all things timing-related in chapter 7, but let's start with understanding ABM segments as the next step. In our experience, having campaign framework segments is critical to be ready to activate.

Targeted Demand Generation: The ownership of this group swings between demand generation and ABM at different companies, but the goal remains the same. Use high-level segments like industries, personas, and geographic locations to target hundreds to thousands of accounts that share traits. This is the broadest level of personalization and spans the widest swath of your market. It is often used as an always-on tier that encompasses email nurtures, content marketing via paid media, and corporate physical and virtual event promotion focused on generating leads. SDR involvement exists in the form of inbound follow-up. This tier should live in parallel with the tiers below. Consider them complementary.

One-to-Many: Likely the most controversial segment in the ABM world, one-to-many exists in many different forms, and there's been much debate as to whether it is truly ABM or not. No ABM police here: If it works for you and your business, it works for us. At Snowflake, we limit this category to time-sensitive plays unique to a specific region or set of regions that are applicable to 50–250 accounts. With personalization technology available today, we can even deliver one-to-one experiences on page load despite this being a one-to-many segment. We will touch more on that later to help you do the same.

One-to-Few: Sometimes your account groupings are too small for a one-to-many approach and too large for one-to-one. This is where one-to-few comes in. At Snowflake, we don't leverage this segment often, but when we do it is for joint-partner programs where we agree on a list of ten to twenty accounts ripe for joint messaging from ourselves and our partner. Alternatively, this could serve as a subset of a one-to-many campaign. For example, you have a healthcare segment and a competitive takeout segment, but the overlap of those two is between ten and fifty accounts. A one-to-few approach works well here to get the message to all relevant parties with the right level of customization for all of them in one fell swoop.

One-to-One: The bread and butter of the account-based world, one-to-one campaigns are the most expensive in terms of time, resources, and financial investment. Yet they are highly effective in delivering unignorable experiences to your buying committee. Because of this, we recommend reserving true one-to-one campaigns for accounts that are high priority but have not responded to broader forms of marketing, have more than ten subsidiaries that require a multi-threading approach; or are make-or-break accounts for your sales leaders' quotas for the year. Account complexity drives the need for multifaceted campaigns focused on a single account. The number of these that you can accommodate depends on the human resources available. We will help you calculate that in the next section.

A general rule of thumb when deciding which campaign segments to use for your account segments is to consider the largest grouping that will still be effective. If you can get the right message to the right people in one-to-many, there is likely no need to invest in a one-to-one strategy for those accounts. Alternatively, if you're working mid–sales cycle with your AE and the account has unique characteristics that you need to address to accelerate the deal, one-to-one is the right option. Other factors, like the number of humans available to create these campaigns and how many reps are intimately involved with the process, will guide how you use each of these.

Now with your TAM defined and your segments labeled, your next task is to divvy up the work internally.

INSIDE THE IGLOO WITH SNOWFLAKE:

John Sapone, senior vice president of US verticals for the North America sales team at Snowflake, on verticals as an organizational advantage for sales teams

Before stepping into his SVP role, John led the Americas Enterprise Sales for Snowflake, a customer-facing organization of over two hundred field personnel that delivered 174 percent year-over-year growth. He also operates as executive customer sponsor for select global leaders in banking, software, insurance and retail, and previously served as vice president of sales for commercial and emerging markets at ServiceNow. Prior to that, he held various executive leadership roles at pre-IPO companies. As a sales executive who has truly seen it all, he balances his analytical, scientific approach to business with equal parts gravitas and humor. John lives in beautiful Atlanta with his wife and three children, and, in his free time, he likes to cook, run, and travel.

We asked him to speak about realigning our internal sales teams to verticals, and how doing so benefited the organization overall.

First, I want to point out a key point of differentiation. You can align your sales team by similar industries, you can get marketing behind it to create some really cool literature, but that's not verticalization. That's segmentation. Verticalization is segmentation plus everything else that comes afterward. The actual dividing of accounts, vertical by vertical, is across other business functions. What about products? What about engineering? Are they building technology that solves verticalized problems? Is legal behind you? Is professional services behind you? When you think about truly deploying a vertical strategy, that's the long tail that everybody forgets about.

On top of that, vertical integration only works at companies with mature customer bases. I've talked to a lot of organizations in the startup phase, or friends of mine that happen to be in the VC world, and I say, "Don't verticalize your business right now. This is a land grab. Unless you can commit the resources, all you're going to do is create a world of haves and have-nots." I believe you have to mature your customer base. Because if I don't have a media company that I can use as a reference for a media vertical, I don't have anything. I want to be able to really cross-pollinate those stories across every industry. As an early stage company, you just can't do that yet.

Now I joined Snowflake in August 2019, and the company was in the midst of trying to decide how to go to market in a much more accelerated fashion. At the time sales was organized by territory, so the first person into a territory had great accounts, the seventh person had every gas station this side of the Mississippi. So there was no rhyme or reason on how to build territories and drive market penetration across every industry. I came in, and my role was to run the enterprise organization; basically every account from 250 employees on up. We went to market and realized quickly that there had been a rush for talent, but not much of a thought process on territories. Ultimately, we saw we had to take a different approach to building our sales organization.

We experimented with addressable markets within territories, but still weren't getting the best results. Fast-forward a couple of years, and I sat down with some other leaders within Snowflake to discuss what was working and what wasn't. We took a bunch of data, and we started analyzing it. And it became glaringly apparent that bringing organizations in that are alike—think alike, buy alike, talk alike—can drive growth in a much more meaningful way faster. If you've got a salesperson that all they do morning, noon, and night is talk about manufacturing, and all of the benefits that Snowflake can drive into a manufacturing organization, they'll get better results. So we started by finding the most influential accounts in a couple of industries and creating verticals around them.

The goal in these verticals was not quantity. It was influence and quality. I said to my team, "I don't want you to have more than forty-five accounts. Our goal, our mission is not more accounts. Our mission is to get aligned by verticals and drive industry-specific solutions."

This is still a fairly recent change, so everyone is still acclimating. But this year, one of the goals I set for my team was to become experts on the industry that they cover. In order to have really relevant meaningful conversations with executives or buyers at any level, you've got to be able to understand the industry. And you've got to be able to articulate how our platform drives real, true business benefits into their specific industry: How it makes them money. How it saves them money. How it mitigates their risk.

Being able to state your opinion with confidence, when you sit in front of an executive, is what really determines whether or not you're going to get the deal. But more importantly, you're going to be viewed as a true partner to them. That's what I want for my team.

Dividing the Work by Group and Capacity

As we've said before, an account-based motion is labor-intensive work. Some of it can definitely be automated, but lots of it cannot; you need smart, eager people with available bandwidth to do this right. And that means that segmentation also comes down to understanding people's working capacities and priorities.

Understanding capacity means working backward from whomever is closest to closed deals. That means you start by considering how many accounts an account executive can reasonably work at one time.

Sales operations is typically the group that runs these calculations, so consult with them. But to generate some rough numbers, estimate how long it takes to close a deal, how many stages there are in a sales cycle, and the activities expected of an AE along the way. Calculate against an eight-hour workday with breaks, and you'll have an idea of how many accounts each AE can manage.

FORMULA: AE Working Hours per Week x 60 / Average Touch Points per Opportunity per Week x Minutes per Touch Point

After AEs come SDRs, since they are the next-closest working group to the closed deals. Assuming your company has at least a few SDRs on staff, you're dealing with a question of ratios: How many AEs should each SDR support?

Travis recommends that growth companies maintain a one-to-one ratio initially, but as the workforce grows, it usually shifts to one SDR supporting three AEs. That ratio can stay constant no matter how large your company gets. This is really a balance of how many AEs an SDR can "handle" and how great the pipeline-generation needs of an AE are. Too many AEs, and an SDR will fail to maintain close alignment. Too few SDRs, and AEs will fail to generate enough pipeline.

Subdividing the work itself means determining how many individuals in an account need to be contacted to start a sales cycle, how many touches need to happen for each of them, and how long it takes to go through those touches. At Snowflake we target SDRs to complete between eighty and one hundred nonautomated touches per eight-hour workday. This is generally applicable to most companies, though less-experienced teams may tackle slightly smaller numbers until they get up to speed.

To get more specific on SDR account capacity, you need to determine:

Contacts per Account: How many individuals within a company do you need to reach out to in order to fully engage the buying committee? Ensure that you factor in the drop-off between those you reach out to and those who actually respond.

Touches per Contact per Week: How many manual (read: nonautomated) touches are you expecting for each contact? We recommend two to three per week.

SDR Workload Capacity: How many manual touches can an SDR execute in a week? At Snowflake we target between eighty and one hundred manual touches per eight-hour workday. This is generally applicable to most companies, though less-experienced teams may tackle slightly smaller numbers.

Plugging these into a formula:

Contacts per Account X Touches per Contact per Week / SDR Workload Capacity

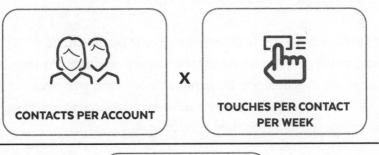

Finally, you need to know how many accounts ABM can reasonably target in any given quarter. Again, this is a matter of ratios, and Hillary prefers to have one ABMer for every twelve to fifteen AEs. (You can do more, but it diminishes your ability to be truly targeted in your outreach efforts. Or you can do less if you are taking a high-touch approach to a very small group of accounts.)

Drilling down a little further:

If your ABM team is doing one-to-many outreach: Each ABMer can usually handle between fifty and one hundred accounts. This is actually drawn from the capacity of the SDR team, since ABMers should only go after accounts that SDRs can support.

If your ABM team is doing one-to-few outreach: Each ABMer can usually handle between ten and fifty accounts. With this type of outreach, ABM needs to be more aligned with the AE's needs since the AE is eager to get a foothold in these accounts but is in need of more intensive support.

If your ABM team is doing one-to-one outreach: Each ABMer can usually handle no more than twenty accounts. At this level, AEs and ABMers are meeting at least once per week, so the ABMer's capacity is mostly determined by how many meetings they can squeeze into their schedules.

If your ABM team is doing a mix of the above: You get to play around with what works best for your team. That is what makes this approach so impactful—you customize the time and resource inputs based on the needs of your account mix. The only magic formula we have here is to try, optimize, and repeat.

At this point, segmenting our market and prioritizing our work-loads together is second nature to us. But we know that's not the case at every company. Plenty of marketing and sales teams either segment separately or not at all . . . and run some serious risks in doing so.

Avoid False Positives, Steward the Trust

You now know all of the advantages of segmenting and how it can improve the work you do. But what happens if you skip this step? Why is it so important that we wrote an entire chapter about it?

We've already alluded to the volume issues that arise without thoughtful segmentation. You end up with more noise than your team can handle. The high volume at the front end leads you to believe you're being productive, but your SDR team learns too late that the prospects they've been chasing are not viable. You've created a leaky funnel brimming with false positives.

Equally important is the fact that attempting one-team GTM without segmentation is exhausting and frustrating. Without the necessary focus to make the work productive, people get burned out, and trust gets broken. Passing accounts to sales and making them do work that clearly isn't valuable makes both parties miserable. If you don't segment wisely, the bridge between sales and marketing may get broken. Segmentation may seem granular and minor, but it truly does help define the alignment path.

So fold segmentation into your workflows and never look back. Then, once you've got a handle on which accounts you're selling to, you can focus on which personas within those accounts deserve your attention. We'll dive into that next.

MINIMUM VIABLE PARAMETERS

Know who your TAM is, which segments are more relevant to your business TODAY.

SCALED PARAMETERS

You have multiple lanes built out (five priority industries), and/or activating on multiples at a time.

MISTAKES TO AVOID

Going after accounts because they're shiny/exciting instead of backed by data. Let data guide which accounts will be most fruitful for sales now.

Don't go after the entire TAM at once and bite off more than you can chew.

Don't let data paralyze you. There's a lot out there. If you over-segment you'll get stuck.

Don't forget to talk with your AE. This will only work if sales and SDRs are on board. If they're not prioritizing an account for any reason, drop it.

5

Know Your Personas by Name

The segments you've just defined will help you divide up your potential customers into manageable, meaningful groups, but to make your account-based motions truly effective you've got to get even more specific. You need to know how your product adds value to each type of customer, inside and outside the office. This is layers beyond the marketing personas that you're used to.

Since the company's inception, Snowflake has been on a mission to be one of the most customer-centric companies in the tech industry. Putting customers first is a company value not only listed transparently on the website, but also one that Snowflake employees are rewarded for modeling. And it doesn't go unnoticed by our customers.

In 2022, 100 percent of Snowflake customer participants in Dresner's market survey said they would recommend Snowflake to other organizations, and that's for the fifth consecutive year.[1] The company also made it onto Forbes' 100 most customer-centric companies of 2022, and to the top ten most customer-centric B2B companies.[2]

This level of customer obsession is largely what makes Snowflake's go-to-market program successful, and customer-centricity is a value we encourage all companies to embrace. It creates a focused space within your marketing efforts to tailor each message and experience to be focused entirely on the customer. In order to do this yourself, you will need to formulate a set of buying personas as your next strategic step in your account-based journey.

Personas Are the Foundation of a One-Team GTM Strategy

In the simplest of terms, a persona is a representation of someone whose problems can be solved by the product or service you're selling. We expect most organizations to have basic personas in place, but basic won't cut it for a hyper-targeted approach. In addition to knowing *who* they are, you need to know *why* they would buy from you. The reason they're so crucial to one-team GTM is that personas help everyone on your team create tailored, targeted outreach to key individuals in efficient and cohesive ways.

In-depth personas are especially powerful because they tie back to motivations: Back in chapter 1 we defined marketing as "a team that drives demand by spreading awareness of products and services at a high level, educating consumers on *why* to buy." If you don't

---

1   Persson, Denise. "The 2022 Snowflake Customer Experience Report." Snowflake. June 13, 2022. https://www.snowflake.com/blog/customer-experience-report-2022/.

2   Morgan, Blake. "The Top 100 Most Customer-Centric Companies of 2022." *Forbes.* May 1, 2022. https://www.forbes.com/sites/blakemorgan/2022/05/01/the-top-100-most-customer-centric-companies-of-2022.

know what's important to people—something you'll learn by building their personas—you can't find or address their why.

Understanding that *why* truly is mandatory when you're selling person-to-person, which means you are taking an account-based angle to begin with. It positions you to approach the people you're contacting at a motivational, psychological level in addition to speaking to them at a professional level. You definitely want to let them know how your offering will help them do well in their job, but if you can also say it will save them time so they can go home and be with their families, or point out that your offering will elevate their work within the business so they're positioned for promotions. You're showing that you know them. And when people feel known, they're more likely to buy.

Much more likely. There's nothing more customer-centric than knowing someone's why and reflecting it back to them in ABM efforts.

Although those key individuals need to feel like they're being spoken to specifically, *you* need to be able to speak to many of them at once as you scale. When you and your team members are familiar with the personas you're addressing, it frees up the ABM and SDR teams to focus on the last mile of personalization. It empowers them to leapfrog into tailoring their message at the account or individual, human levels. Said another way, you save your team members from trying to figure out what a data engineer generally cares about, and instead home their aperture in on what specific data pipelines matter to Emily Engineer at Happy Healthcare.

Personas are detailed and specific, but they're also a form of standardization. Having them in place enables you to do quality control on your work and monitor performance more easily. For example, once you've built out a persona for "data scientist," you'll be able to:

Create variants instead of rebuilding from scratch (data scientist at a healthcare company, data scientist at a media company, etc.)

Ensure all messages sent to data scientists are appropriately worded and properly calibrated (provide a consistent customer experience)

Create metrics that apply to every data scientist in that persona group

Measure and optimize what works for anyone who fits that persona

On top of all these reasons, if you *didn't* take the time to create some robust personas and you still wanted to personalize your outreach, you'd be reinventing the wheel for every single person you contacted. That doesn't scale very well. You're better off doing the work now, categorizing the people whose pain you can alleviate and sorting them into small, well-defined groups.

Now that you're thoroughly convinced, let's dive into building those personas.

What You Need to Know about Your Personas (and Why)

Persona formulation is a practice that's been around for decades, and other experts may recommend other approaches, but here's how we suggest building an initial set for your account-based practice. As you go through this exercise, keep your own internal customer in mind. What does an SDR *need* to know as they craft a personal email? What's nice to have, but not actually core to the experience that an ABM specialist is building? If you already have a rock-solid handle on personas, feel free to skip ahead to the next section.

Role+: Understanding their role within their company and how your product is relevant to them on the business side will help you frame your messages to really hit home. Don't just include pain points, but also things they could do better, gaps, and opportunities. All of these offer you ways of communicating the value of your offering in ways that will truly resonate.

Titles and Aliases: A list of titles this persona might be known by is vitally important, because one role may have multiple different titles across various industries.

Tenure: This is routinely glossed over, but knowing average tenure is a strategic must. Say you're selling to a CMO, and their average tenure is two and a half years. If you have a one-year buying cycle and a one-year contract, you're likely going to get ripped out the following year. That means your messaging needs to address how you can help them extend their tenure. How are you going to help them break that mold?

How They Get Information: What publications do they read, both print and online? Do they belong to professional associations or clubs? Where do they go to understand how to become better at their job? Knowing this can help you decide where to reach them with targeted ads and also give you insight into what problems they are trying to solve in their daily work.

Role in Buying Committee: As we've said, most buying is done by committees. If the CFO is the last stop in the process, someone else is the first stop. Often an individual contributor, or the end user, is the best entry point to a conversation. Knowing what influence each person has in the overall process will help you create messaging that connects the overall value of your product across the decision-makers and influencers.

Performance Metrics: How is their performance measured? What markers of success or failure do they rely on? How are they paid or compensated? This also feeds into whether this person is typically measured on day-to-day tactics or strategic business outcomes.

In past experiences, we have also included a stock image of a person for each of our personas. We want to capture things like average age, demographics, and working environment (C-suite or a server room?). You may also want to give each persona a name: Data Scientist Dave, CIO Carly, etc. These may seem like granular details, but they will help your team members remember and relate to these personas whenever they call them up in your database.

WORK PROFILE	CONTENT/ENGAGEMENT PROFILE
Title(s)/Pay Range	Go-To Source of Information
Average Tenure/Seniority/YOE	Preferred Content Type (technical vs. business, etc.)
Org Structure Up + Down	Preferred Content Format (ebook, video, etc.)
KPIs	Preferred Content Length
What will get them promoted/fired?	Content Volume

Build out 1 slide per persona as a quick reference. Think about it as telling a story about your buyer.

To generate truly useful personas, we also recommend doing a few customer interviews. Pick up the phone, call a customer that you sold to six months ago, and ask them two questions: What was the thing that made you want to spend money with us in the first place? And what have you discovered about using our product in the last six months that surprised and delighted you? Plug their answers back into your personas so you can surface it in your messaging.

Talking with actual customers is especially valuable during persona-building, because it reminds you that the people you're selling to may be very different from you. Their experiences and pain points may surprise you, if you take the time to ask about them. Talking to your customers will always make your work better and more effective.

Sales and Marketing Must Align on Persona Messaging

Most companies are doing multi-touch marketing right now, but they are doing it in a disconnected way. They're letting marketing and sales teams stay in their silos, operating without communicating, which means the messages they send have no unifying threads to tie them together. We believe that success in multi-touch, ABM-style marketing only comes with connection and alignment. And that includes alignment around personas.

Elise Bergeron, Vice President of Product Marketing and Community at Snowflake, insists that getting sales and marketing on the same page for personas is mandatory. She says, "The benefit of ABM is we have the ability to dive deeper than your average demand-gen motion. We sit with sales, and together we determine how to tweak that message for a specific person with a specific title. That allows us to be a little bit more granular than the broader marketing motion."

That granularity is critical. In addition to a profile that contains their title, average tenure, and other details, you'll need a well-defined core message for each persona. Multi-touch integrated motions rely on sending a consistent message to the people you're contacting. If you want to give them a good customer experience—which, of course, you do—you need to send them the same message repeated in different forms and across different media so it has time to become memorable and fully resonate.

If your company is early in its development, working on core messages for your personas will mean getting sales and marketing in a room, making a grid of people you sell to (or want to sell to), then talking to early customers to beef up your initial drafts. Within more mature companies, product marketing usually creates and finalizes the core message for each persona, but it does so with lots of input and updates from sales and the SDR team. The final core messages are usually included as part of a more robust solution-selling enablement. These lengthy documents are critical for the sellers to understand how and why your solution helps the prospect, but can be convoluted for marketers to use at scale. This is why we recommend creating a simplified version of the output for GTM teams to use in their daily campaign creation.

In what we like to call "The Magic Matrix," we distill the key value added to each persona into a core message, then translate it into short- and long-form copy. Most people jump straight to copy creation and miss the core message. This is a critical step, because if the core message, the piece that makes your messaging truly customer-centric, is not solid, the rest of your copy and therefore applications of it will not be successful.

CORE MESSAGE

	Why they should care? IMPACT	Intent Keywords and/or SEO	Ad Copy	Relevant Case Study	Prospect Sequence
Persona 1					
Persona 2					
Industry 1					
Industry 2					

ADD COMPLEXITY AFTER BASELINE IS ESTABLISHED

Example of custom content

Map out how the value add for each persona translates to keywords, copy content and sales activation material BEFORE launching any programs. This is your key to scaling later.

To bring this process to life in your own organization, we recommend:

Start with whatever existing persona information you have, likely in the form of sales enablement material.

Take your best shot at creating one or two sentences of core message for each persona, focused on the business outcomes they will experience, *not* the speeds and feeds of the product.

Take that core message to cross-functional groups including product marketing and sales. Review and adjust until you agree.

Start creating marketing copy in short and long form that is based on the core message you agreed upon.

Use this matrix to create consistency of messaging across ABM and SDR activations.

When you are ready to scale, repeat the process for more granular drill-downs of your personas. Create one per persona per industry.

These core messages for each persona will permeate your content library and therefore your SEO strategy, advertising, and web copy, as well as outbound prospecting messages across channels. They're the thread that ties every piece of your ABM, SDR, and sales efforts together. Without them, you'll send disconnected messages that confuse your buyers, muddle your value propositions, and prevent you from effectively scaling your campaigns.

Turning Your Personas into People

Now that you've done the work of segmenting the companies you want to target and bucketed the relevant personas who operate in those companies, you need a solution for building your database of contacts. Just like you can't ask an SDR or AE to call a segment, you can't ask them to call a persona. You need to curate details about the people who work at the accounts you want to engage with.

We recommend starting with an audit of your existing database to understand how many people with the titles and job functions you have already. In fact, not just how many you have, but how many you have per targeted account and how many of those are marketable. (We define "marketability" as contacts who are eligible to receive marketing communications; they have opted in in the countries that require it, or have *not* opted out.) If you are going to take an account-based approach, you not only need relevant contacts in general, but you need them within the specific accounts you plan to activate.

With gaps identified, you can take one (or all) of these three routes to filling them:

> **Pay to Supplement:** Take a look at the landscape of data providers out there. There are loads of companies who offer B2B contact info that can be valuable to you, including email addresses, current and past job titles, and more. One key recommendation is to "layer" data providers on top of each other. One provider may provide excellent coverage in North America, while another excels in the Asia-Pacific region. Also do your homework before expending any of your budget: Make sure your vendors acquire their data ethically and legally, and that any information you're buying meets the regulatory requirements of any countries where you plan to market.

Outsource Contact Discovery: Any list from a data provider will have holes of its own and the inherent limitation of becoming stale, so you may not be able to fill all of your critical gaps just by purchasing a list. Fortunately there are other providers who will call key people, do custom research on social media and public websites, and manually curate relevant lists for your target accounts. Depending on your available time and budget and the specificity of your personas, it can be wise to outsource the work of manually augmenting your database.

Attract Contacts to Opt In: Ongoing demand gen is also a path to building your database. The "wide net" we discussed in the introduction definitely has its limits, but it is effective at getting individuals to opt in to the database. Bear in mind, though, that you need to collect and handle this data carefully, or you run the risk of violating CAN-SPAM regulations, the General Data Protection Regulation, or other privacy laws. Treat people's data with care, because you'll use it to fuel your outbound motions.

At Snowflake we use all three of these methods for augmenting our own data. And once we've got a persona fully realized, we use it across multiple sales and marketing groups to make sound decisions and create effective campaigns. We translate the personas (internal sketches of *types of people*) into contacts (real people we'd like to contact).

ABM segments contacts to determine which ads/digital experiences/content to show to which people.

Event marketing uses the database to decide who to invite to their live events.

SDRs use contacts to determine which sequences to send.

INSIDE THE IGLOO WITH SNOWFLAKE:

Elise Bergeron, vice president of product marketing and communities at Snowflake, on the importance of personas

Elise Bergeron is a marketing executive with experience spanning startups to public companies. She currently serves as vice president of product marketing and communities at Snowflake. Elise joined Snowflake via the acquisition of Stride, a customer data platform, where she was cofounder and COO. Prior to Stride, she led marketing for SalesforceIQ and what is now Salesforce Einstein as VP of marketing at Salesforce. She has also held product marketing and management roles at Facebook, Amazon, and Vistaprint (Cimpress). Elise has an MBA from Harvard Business School and a BA from Stanford University.

We asked her to speak about why personas matter across marketing and sales functions and how she uses them in her own work.

Marketing is about connecting with your audience and figuring out how to speak to them in a way that is relevant, adds value, and helps them understand why they should care about whatever you're selling. Personas are the formal way we define who that audience is.

One of the first steps our team takes to define personas is to consider our go-to-market framework. It's an important way to lay groundwork. How are you orienting yourself toward the market? How do you define your offering? Who do you want to use your product? Who are all of the people who could get value from your product? You have to map that information and create some sort of architecture to think about how all these people fit together. How do all the pieces of your story fit together?

Once you've done that mapping exercise, then you start clicking within that and saying, "Now let's take each of these roles and build out an understanding of them." Who is this person and what do they care about? What are the titles that would typically cover this role? What are their responsibilities? Who do they work with in an organization? What skills do they have? And fundamentally, the most important question is, what are their goals? And what are their pain points? Because those are what's actually going to drive a marketing and selling motion.

Finally, we think about our best positioning angle relative to this particular audience. What are the competitive considerations? What do you need to know when you're addressing this audience? What are they hearing from others? And then therefore, what do we show them? What are the capabilities we should talk about? What are the benefits we should talk about? And what's the differentiation?

Finding the right level of granularity for personas is critical. If you go too broad, there's no value there, because even though two people might have similar titles on paper, they actually have totally different skills. So the value prop you offer would need to be totally different for each of them.

On the other hand if you go too fine grain, it just becomes useless. There's probably twenty different titles underneath data engineer, but building a persona for each is a waste of your time. The challenge with personas is always figuring out how to go deep and specific enough without getting overly granular. To find that happy medium, you need to constantly test your personas. Ask, "Is this specific enough to be insightful and actionable? And is it rolled up enough so people can use it without getting overwhelmed or freezing up?"

It takes some trial and error, but I also believe that most marketers should have reasonable intuition around finding that balance.

Personas may seem like helpful-but-optional tools, but believe us when we say that your account-based efforts will struggle without them. Building multidimensional personas and attaching core messages to them is vital work. If you don't have them in place before you forge ahead, you'll find it impossible to write engaging, effective content for the people you most need to reach. You won't understand them, and that means you'll miss the mark.

So before you turn the page and dig into our guidance around building content, make sure you know exactly what's driving Data Scientist Dave and CIO Carly. It's knowledge that will serve you well.

MINIMUM VIABLE PERSONA
Titles, responsibilities, pain points/opportunities that your product can solve

SCALED PERSONA
Have the infrastructure for personas with core messages aligned so you can replicate them across industries and roles.

MISTAKES TO AVOID
Don't go too broad or too narrow: aim for a healthy balance of detail.

Don't assume that you know your personas well enough without going through the exercise of creating them fully. You probably don't know all of the relevant details off the top of your head.

Don't make yourself into your persona.

Don't skip this step. Personas are incredibly important.

6

Design a Hyper-Targeted Content Ecosystem

Although we've only referenced it obliquely so far, content sits at the heart of any account-based program. Quality writing, eye-catching graphics, perfectly personalized emails, and engaging landing pages are all elements of this work, and you're nearly ready to start planning and building a library of your own content.

But first, a quick note about how and why content has developed a critical role in B2B go-to-market motions.

Decades ago, some companies would create "advertorials," publish magazine-catalog hybrids, or find other ways to marry sales messages and content, but most marketing was pretty straightforward. Ads looked like ads, and informational content looked quite different. But when the internet became a giant, global marketplace, that dynamic shifted. What started as corporate websites sharing content designed to build awareness and foster brand affinity evolved into complex SEO strategies and multiarmed social media campaigns.

But the motivation is the same: Marketers and salespeople know that people resist the hard-sell approach and react better to approaches that make them feel seen and valued. Buyers would rather spend as much time as they need researching and making decisions than feel coerced, and the slow drip of content marketing gives them space to do that.

Josh Braun—an influencer in the sales space and a trainer we use at Snowflake—has a fantastic analogy to describe the dynamics of content marketing. He says that building trust with a sales prospect is all about making deposits: offering them valuable information, showing them shortcuts and little-known resources, giving away free goodies to show that you're honestly invested in supporting them. Braun says you need to make many deposits before you can approach the "withdrawal" that is a sales request.[1] Content marketing—via ABM or other programs—is the perfect vehicle for making a slew of super-targeted deposits before finally circling around to that withdrawal request.

But it can only be successful at that level if it's strategically implemented and systematically organized. So let's talk about building a robust content ecosystem within your company.

Content Must Be Personalized *and* Relevant

As you move into designing your content ecosystem, remember that the emails you write and account experiences you design don't just need to be personalized, *they must also be relevant*. It's not enough to show the recipient that you know who they are and what they want; you also need to speak to the challenges they're facing right now, in this exact moment. Relevancy is a delicate dance of timing,

---

1   Braun, Josh. "Less Withdrawals, More Deposits." Josh Braun. https://joshbraun.com/overdrawn/.

message, and experience. When done in harmony, it tells a story that resonates. When ignored, it can make an otherwise well-calibrated message fall flat.

The best way to ensure relevance is by solidifying the core value messaging we discussed in chapter 5 and speaking to it across media. Instead of slapping a company name on a topic-relevant web page as personalization, relevancy looks like including five to seven pieces of content on that microsite that speak to different elements of their business (think tech stack, partners, and company references from industry peers) and CTAs that match their stage of the buying cycle (ex: Book a meeting with your expert vs. join our community). In addition, one of the most critical factors is timing: If your target account signed a deal with your competitor last week, otherwise-relevant content becomes meaningless. If you reach out the month before their contract with your competitor ends, you will make a much bigger impact.

We will get more into timing in chapter 7, but wanted to preview it here since it ties strongly to relevance. Keep this in mind when you create templates for content: the ability to tweak, add, and customize is critical to ensuring your content speaks to readers and recipients in a timely manner.

Start Your Content Library with Existing Assets

To begin populating your content library for your account-based motion, you should start with existing content that you already have. Either adjust it or organize it in a way that makes sense based on what you now know about your personas and your customers' buying journey. We find that starting with an audit of everything from existing blog posts and newsletters to customer stories, thought leadership content, video snippets from demos, animated short-form content, recorded webinars, and virtual events works best. Anything that's well-written or was well received by your customer base can usually be transformed into the foundation for a new account-based campaign. In fact, if there is a component of content that is still relevant and represents your value-add well, but it lives in an otherwise lackluster or out-of-date asset, mark it for later. You can come back and extract the still-valuable elements and bring them to life in new content in the future. This is especially valuable for startups that are lean on content and need to repurpose it to add variety and bulk.

You can also enrich and add to your current crop of content so it aligns with newer strategies that you're building inside your organization. But whatever you do, start by identifying gaps to see what you can repurpose before generating any net-new content. No need to start from zero when you undoubtedly have a wealth of content that can be repurposed.

Organize Content into Categories

Once you've got a collection of content possibilities, begin labeling and organizing them. At the broadest level, all the content in your ecosystem should fall into three buckets based on the buyer's journey:

Problem Education: How is this problem going to affect the recipient and why should they care? Assume they didn't know they needed to worry about it and you are informing them for the first time. This should not have product content in it; it is strictly a "deposit," as Josh Braun would say.

Solution Research: Now that they know the issue exists, what are the potential solutions on the market? Touch on product-related content at the concept level, but not at the granular level. You can introduce the brand's value proposition, but do not sell here.

Solution Selection: Your buyer understands the challenge and the possible solutions. Now they need to understand why your company is the best solution to choose. This is where you can go all in with solution briefs, speeds and feeds, etc.

We're grateful to Harvard Business School lecturer Mark Roberge, who defined these categories in his book *The Sales Acceleration Formula*. We feel that dividing content in this way is far more practical than using the typical content "funnel" concept.

When we think "top of funnel," most marketers think of very broad brand awareness messaging. But in many cases, the buyer doesn't need to know about your brand yet . . . they need to be educated about a specific problem and understand whether or not they are suffering from it. (They may not know that slow web page load times are abnormal and need to understand that they're abnormal first before they will care that your high-speed internet service brand exists.)

After Problem Education comes Solution Research, because jumping right to product information will make people feel pressured and rushed. Giving potential customers the full scope of options to solve the problem you already established is an important step. However, most companies mistakenly jump straight to the last stage, touting why their product is the best option.

Only then, at Solution Selection, does it make sense to offer information about speeds, feeds, technical specs, and solution briefs so the buyer understands that *your* solution is the one they should select. Roberge's categories create this customer-centric framework right from the start.

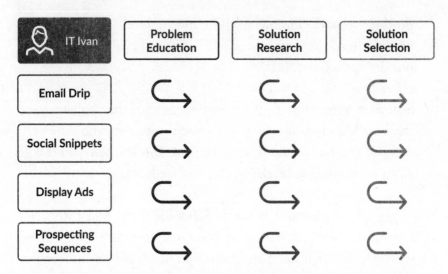

By organizing your content into Roberge's three categories, you will create a full-funnel content machine to execute by channel. You can now activate that content across personas in an email-drip for example, to take your buyer through a relevant narrative. Tune into chapter 8 for more on when to trigger these.

INSIDE THE IGLOO WITH SNOWFLAKE:

Jackie Kiler, senior director of demand generation at Snowflake, on how to build a top-notch content ecosystem

Jackie is a B2B marketing expert with twenty years of experience in demand generation, event marketing, partner marketing, and growth marketing. She leads the demand-generation function of more than thirty team members at Snowflake, where she is responsible for campaigns from conception to execution. During her six-year tenure at Snowflake, she has helped scale the revenue engine from $50M to over $1 billion.

We asked her to speak about where to start building your content library and a few pitfalls to avoid.

Building a quality content ecosystem must start with identifying your ideal customer profile. In doing that, you also identify the pain points for that customer, which helps you determine which topics you should address in the content.

Then as you start adding to your library, you want to ensure that you have content at each stage of the journey. Problem education content is designed to get people to think about whether they have a certain problem and why. Those content pieces may focus more on industry trends than specific solutions. Then, assuming they have the problem, you move them into solution research content, which discusses how they could potentially fix it. At that level you're working with customer case studies, quick starts, and webinars. Finally, you offer them solution selection content, which urges them to take action on your product. That's the final phase and the one where you talk most about features.

Creating content for all three stages is critical, but you also have to realize that people are going to enter the content journey wherever they feel most comfortable. They'll poke in at phase 3, and then they'll go back out. They might do their own research offline. They're going to be engaging with content on different platforms and talking with other people. The way to address that unpredictability is by making sure your content ecosystem covers a range of topics and offers multiple different types of content delivery tactics.

Some people really like to read, some prefer demos, others need a combination. I suggest including instructor-led and self-led options. Let people learn about things step-by-step or through an e-book or a blog. Use different content types to address each individual content, objective, or topic. When you do this, it allows people to engage wherever they want and still come away with valuable information.

The great thing is that most quality content can be repurposed across formats. I would always start with a webinar. It's easier for people to put slides together than write a full e-book.

And for problem education, I would always start with numbers: Five ways to do something, eight signs you need to upgrade, etc. Those are usually much more engaging when you're promoting them on digital platforms. Once you have a webinar, you can turn it into an e-book, then you turn it into a blog, then put together a video demo. If you choose your topics well and understand the people who are interested in your solution, you can transform anything into multiple high-quality pieces of content.

Organize and Tag Content

After sorting into those initial categories, it's a matter of examining each piece of content through a series of lenses that are relevant to your buyer. A system with multiple layers of labels is practical, since these lenses have a lot of overlap. There are several systems available to make this possible, from simple spreadsheets to robust document repositories or content experience platforms. Regardless of your mechanism, having a single library or reference with assets and their coordinating tags will be critical to scaling your ABM program later. The basic, fundamental tags we suggest include:

Persona: Which persona(s) align best with the content? This should be limited to one persona per asset.

Industry: Which primary industry is the content tailored for?

Solution: Which of your company's solutions/offerings/products does this asset support?

Journey Stage: Does this piece of content help with problem education, solution research, or solution selection? If there is no journey stage aligned, this is your hint to reconsider how you are writing content.

Additional: You can add additional tags relevant to your business, but be careful not to overcomplicate. Remember, the results are only as good as the system, and if the system is overly complicated, it will break down. If any of the tags are not relevant, create an option for "No Persona," "No Industry," etc. This way the person reviewing any given entry will know the tags were left out intentionally as opposed to by mistake.

Now that you have your content organized, you need to determine what opportunities are available to you to personalize your base content, by channel. We like to think of this like a Venn diagram. When you list your channels in one set of circles and your areas of personalization in another, where do they overlap?

Personalization: Evaluate if messaging, content, or experience can be personalized further by industry, decision stage, competitor, or tech stack if appropriate for the target group.

Channel: How do you plan to reach out to the target group? What makes the most sense considering what you want to tell them? SDR touch points? Marketing emails? Each channel lends itself to a different suite of personalization opportunities.

Data Source: Some personalization points are straightforward at a small scale, like company name and industry. However, as you grow your program and add in elements of orchestration, you'll need a reliable data source to populate personalized elements. We recommend mapping out what data you have available to power your personalization.

| | Delivery | | | | | Data | | |
	Content	SDR Sequences	Content Experience	Paid Media	Marketing Emails	Intent Data	Journey Stage	Engaged Data
Account	Segment + Company name	Segment + Company name	Segment + Company name	Segment + Company name	Segment + Company name	Segment + Intel	Segment	Segment
Industry	Content + Graphics	Use case, Business value	Text + Graphics + Content	Text + Graphics + Targeting	Text + Graphics + Targeting	Surging Industry topics	Additional use cases for industry	Buying centers in account
Solution	Content + Graphics	Use Case + PBOs	Text + Graphics + Content	Text + Graphics	Graphics + PBOs	Which solution to focus on	X-sell opp, customize content	Insight into which solution
Persona	PBOs	Role + Title + Use cases + PBOs	Content, Chat bot	Graphics + Message	Graphics + Message	Role-related surges	Identify new LOB for customers	Insight into new LOBs who to focus on

Relevancy

Identify the overlap of your channels and opportunities for relevancy to narrow in on your sweet spot for personalization.

This part of the process—sorting and categorizing all of your content pieces—is a bit like organizing the pieces of a jigsaw puzzle. If they're all in a big messy pile, it'll take you longer to determine how they can fit together. But if you sort them by type or color (or both), you've got a much more informed starting point. You can use the grid we provided above as a simple worksheet for mapping out your content, how you can personalize it, and your data sources.

We'll dive into using your content to plan strategic account-based plays in the coming chapter, but for now just focus on gathering, creating, and categorizing your content. Doing this first will make creating strategies and launching customer experiences much, much easier.

Most of the content pieces we've discussed up to this point fall on the marketing and ABM team member side, but the SDR team can also create a ready-made resource pool to draw upon. Let's look at how to build one.

Refining Your Sequence Library

Landing pages, visualizations, and case studies are typically created and managed by teams within the marketing department, and sales relies on those creative outputs to enable their work. For SDR teams, this comes in the form of the all-important sequence: the touch pattern of emails, calls, social connections, and other outreach that defines what, when, and how SDRs engage with contacts. Many companies struggle to create the necessary structure needed to make sequences truly valuable, falling into the trap of treating them as simple email automation or something that SDRs should figure out for themselves. Getting your sequences right will make or break your SDRs' effectiveness in executing on an ABM strategy. This is why we can confidently say that sales engagement platforms, which maintain these sequences, have become fundamentally more important than CRM (customer relationship management) when it comes to SDR teams.

As you might expect, the sequence library in a sales engagement platform should never be managed in a vacuum: Everything in it must dovetail with any content pieces being created and refined by marketing. Otherwise you risk sending disjointed messages, confusing your buyers, and missing out on that all-important one-two punch of ABM and SDR combined. So be sure to align all content creation and library-building between marketing and sales.

At Snowflake, we create this alignment through what we call a "content committee." This is a group composed of SDRs, product marketers, sales executives, and other subject matter experts (where necessary). A cross-functional group, this committee guides the content process by sharing diverse insights and perspectives, and we had to bust a few silos to create it. The committee can start as a core group of an SDR manager, product marketer, and your best salesperson. This provides the respective expertise of how to craft excellent prospecting messages, how to capture your company's core value propositions, and how to demonstrate the social proof and expertise that resonates in front of customers.

The committee is directed by SDR leadership and has exclusive permission to publish sequences that the rest of the organization can view and use. That's right, we recommend locking down sequence-creation from everyone except the members of this committee. The alternative is letting entropy take its course. When anyone and everyone can develop their own "content," you find yourself in the Wild West: duplicating efforts, missing best practices, sharing outdated value propositions, and ultimately creating "sequence sprawl" where the business loses all sense of what content is actually working. Thankfully sales engagement platforms have the ability to prescribe governance roles to different types of users, so your content pros can focus on building while your end users focus on bringing human-powered value to the market.

In terms of the sequence library itself, you should aim for a set of sequences that speak to the primary factors that change your value proposition. For example, if you sell to five distinct personas that each have three distinct value propositions, you could start out with a library of fifteen sequences to account for these combinations. It's okay to add more sequences over time as the content committee triages requests from sales and marketing, but remember that the content in sequences themselves can and will be customized by SDRs to each account and/or individual. That is where the power of the SDR really comes in: taking the thoughtful segmentation work that's been done and tailoring the "last mile" of the message to the accounts that they have personally researched.

At Snowflake, our sequences typically start with heavier personalization and more manual effort by the SDR to build credibility and make "deposits" with the contact. Then the communication shifts toward semiautomated and automated calls to action that give the contact the most relevant next step, whether that be a meeting with sales, an invitation to an event, or a sign-up for a free trial. This structure is one of many best practices that will maximize your effectiveness with sequences. Here are our other favorites:

Force personalization in certain email templates by inserting directions for how the SDR should tailor the messaging.

Subject lines should not exceed a few relevant words.

Avoid single-channel sequences (e.g., 100 percent automated emails with no calls or manual steps).

Write Compelling Email Templates:

Personalization: Include an account-specific or person-specific trigger (compelling event like their job posting) or background info (the fact they worked at a company that is a customer).

Relevant value: Position your company and explain why they would specifically care about it.

Call to action: Ask for a specific time to meet in a natural way, or offer an alternative next step such as a webinar or free trial.

Emails should be very brief, but packed with value.

Throttle the number of contacts that can be activated in a sequence in a twenty-four-hour window.

Give contacts "breathing room" by spacing out sequence steps in a professionally persistent manner.

Above all, remember that all of the content and sequencing in your sales engagement platform must be cohesive and aligned. If you put all the work into organizing your content on the marketing side, your impact will only reach so far if you're not connected on the sales side. Be sure to continue busting silos as you begin creating and organizing content. Everything you're building is related and connected and should be organized in a way that makes that clear. When it is—and when your ABM work sets the stage for SDRs to follow up and get people into meetings—the amplification is unbeatable. It truly does feel like 1 + 1 = 3.

Exciting, right? So next, let's make that amplification happen by planning out your initial plays.

MINIMUM VIABLE ECOSYSTEM
Content at all three stages of the funnel

Lock down sequence template creation, create a library.

SCALED ECOSYSTEM
Content across all three stages for each buying persona and industry

Know what paths to more personalization are.

Introduce new channels like video and direct mail on the SDR side.

MISTAKES TO AVOID
Don't feel compelled to use all content that exists.

Don't forge ahead without knowing your end goal.

Build your case and gather data points over time instead of trying to win over naysayers right from the start.

PART 3
HOW

7

Calculate Timing (Unless You Don't Need To)

In part 1, we explained why unification of sales and marketing is the best possible way to build a GTM motion. Then in part 2, we discussed how to find the right accounts to target and how to define and organize your messages. Now, in part 3, you'll learn how to deliver those messages at the right time.

In 2020, amid the COVID-19 pandemic, we had an "aha" moment about a simple concept: timing.

We were tracking companies who'd shown interest in Snowflake through online activities using an intent data vendor. Using this data, we compiled lists of possible accounts to pursue and shared them with sales. We noticed something interesting: An online travel company was showing a surge of interest in data science and engineering platforms during the COVID-19 pandemic. This account was assigned to a salesperson and squarely in Snowflake's TAM, but we were not paying much attention to it given that the travel industry was struggling due to the global lockdown. Why would we point our outbound marketing machine at a company that was probably hemorrhaging money?

But because we saw their interest in the data, we decided to spin up a play together targeting this company with a simple microsite focused on the topics of interest, coupled with the one-two punch of SDR messaging about our customer stories in the travel industry. With the AE aligned, after just a couple of tries, we not only secured a meeting with this travel company, we found out they were three months into a proof of concept with one of our biggest competitors!

It turns out that they were looking for a solution to help predict and surface offers to their customers so they could stay ahead in the fast-moving landscape of the pandemic. This opened up an opportunity for our sales team to position our product's data science capabilities head-to-head. We ended up signing on the customer in half the typical time.

Had we reached out a couple of months later, we'd be asking how well our competitor's implementation was going. That's the importance of timing.

Timing literally determines whether or not your message will be heard or fall on deaf ears. The concept of right timing isn't hard to grasp but does take skill and coordination to act upon, especially at scale. This chapter will illustrate the best practices of how to determine the iron is hot and when to strike.

Some accounts may totally ignore your marketing messages for years because they're simply not ready to listen, much less buy. But when they *become* ready, you need to be aware of that shift. When you find evidence that they're in the market, curious, investigating . . . it's time to swoop in and educate them on why they should work with you. Give them that personalized, highly relevant information at the right moment, and you've got a great shot at success.

When you know how to interpret the signals, you can insert yourself. You can get a seat at the table with customers who might not even have known you existed before you reached out to them.

We also acknowledge that there are accounts you have to go after regardless of timing: the "must win" logos of the business. But even those accounts can be approached strategically by monitoring timing-adjacent factors, as we'll explain later in this chapter.

But for now, we'll focus on the companies that make up the bulk of your TAM, where you need to be judicious with your focus and strike when opportunity presents itself. For these target accounts, *timing drives relevance*. At Snowflake, we assign sales territories, initiate outbound campaigns, and spend marketing dollars based on the engagements we are monitoring across a single, unified view of the TAM in our CRM and data warehouse.

As Josh Braun often tells our SDR onboarding classes, "Your potential customers are getting the job done today without you. They are getting from point A to B. It's not your job to get their motivation to change, it's your job to align with it."[1] That motivation to change could come from many places: a sudden shift within their industry, a current vendor falling down when it counts, or a new executive ushering in a new strategic vision. It is possible to sell without aligning to these events, but you radically amplify your message when you harmonize with the journeys of your customers-to-be. Think about what happens when the frequency of a sound matches the resonant frequency of a champagne glass.

---

1 Braun, Josh. "Are You Chasing?" Josh Braun. https://joshbraun.com/are-you-chasing/.

We see this approach as an evolution of the concept of "inbound marketing" which was first articulated by HubSpot cofounder Brian Halligan back in 2005.[2] This strategy focuses on a "pull" approach to marketing, where you set up your online presence in a way that attracts visitors naturally through search engines, blogging, social media, and all manner of digital content. Even though inbound depends on the customer finding you and outbound asks you to find the customer, both strategies benefit tremendously from timing. It is a universal (yet obvious) truth of sales and marketing that you have a better chance of selling your product if your potential customer currently has a reason to buy it.

So how do you learn the art of timing? How can you determine when the time is right to begin warming up an account? The answer can be found where we started this chapter: intent data.

Elements of Timing

We like to think of marketing and sales as a two-way street. Instead of a company's marketing and sales teams constantly flooding customers with information and sales pitches regardless of circumstances, we need to listen to what those customers are telling us. Are they dissatisfied with their current tools or services? Interested in what we're selling, but unable to buy right now? Badgering people makes them dislike you and tune out your messages. Responding to the signals they're sending out makes them feel seen and heard.

Those signals are intent: the collection of behaviors that tells you when the other party is showing interest in your offering, subject, or area of expertise.

---

2   "Helping millions grow better." Hubspot. https://www.hubspot.com/our-story.

Back in chapter 3 we talked a bit about intent data—activities that show us where an account is situated in the buying cycle—but we'll dive deeper now. Think of intent data like a compass, pointing you to the accounts and personas most likely to accelerate the growth path of your business. For net-new acquisition, this could be the direction you need for prioritization; which accounts are most likely to respond now versus later? For large, complex accounts with multiple buying centers and subsidiaries, intent can point you to *which* subsidiary or *which* line of business is the best place to target based on specific keywords or personas. Similarly, in customer accounts, intent can help you determine the right time to pitch a cross-sell opportunity, to which department, based on changing behavioral signals within the product and research they are doing online.

It's an inspection metric that we use at the top of our account funnel; a signal that tells us if we make a move now, we'll be reaching out exactly when an account is most likely to be interested in our offerings. There's a widespread misconception that intent is limited to web research, but this simply isn't true: Intent data encompasses a variety of signals. We consider everything from responses to our marketing campaigns to product-usage data and third-party content consumption. Regardless of how you use intent, sales, marketing and SDRs should all be a part of the data review and account selection in order to take a one-team approach.

Intent data can be broken down into two categories.

First-party intent data: This is activity data that your company owns and has access to and that is relevant to your contacts. It includes firmographic, technographic, and behavioral data. It helps you answer this question: How likely is this account to further engage with your marketing and sales efforts based on the behavior they are exhibiting on *your own* properties?

First-party intent data includes:

Web traffic: When people visit your website, are they doing so from an IP address owned by a potential customer company? Meaning, if you are hoping to land Netflix as a customer, are employees with Netflix company IPs engaging with content on your website?

Engagement with marketing: Are individuals from your target accounts showing up at your field events or clicking through on your digital advertisements? Interacting with your existing campaigns can be an indication of interest and therefore trigger customized ABM outreach.

Engagement with sales: Email opens, email replies, and answering SDR calls are all signals of intent. In these cases we're looking specifically for reciprocated touch points: They don't just receive your point of contact: they opened, replied, or both.

Product telemetry: Intent can be tracked by monitoring existing usage of your product/solution. Is anyone from a target account using a free trial? Are they using one feature, but might benefit from another?

Competitive renewals: Let's say your sales team had a call with a prospect account, and learned that they just bought from a competitor. Instead of accepting defeat, this data point becomes a banked intent signal that can be revisited at the new contract's end date. The ABM team can set a calendar reminder to circle back in a year when the prospect will be renewing.

Depending on the number and strength of these signals, one or more should trigger a one-team play against that account. That said, you may want to augment the free first-party data your company can access with external sources of third-party intent data.

Third-party intent data is activity data supplied by external sources that's highly relevant to your contacts. You're looking for an abnormal increase in behavior signals *outside* your company's properties that indicate a buying cycle is approaching or indicate that some other change is imminent that could pave the way for a sale. It helps you answer this question: How likely is this account to further engage with your marketing and sales efforts based on the behavior they are exhibiting on *external* properties?

Third-party intent data includes:

Third-party research activity: The type and frequency of research that accounts in your TAM are conducting gives you a window into their forthcoming intentions. Using tools like Natural Language Processing, you can look for an abnormal surge in research on websites other than your own. For example, are a growing number of people at a target account consuming content related to a competitor? If so, they may not even realize your business is an option! Now you know which business area to contact, and which competitor's name you should drop to grab their attention.

Job changes: We often refer to this as "champion tracking." When someone at an existing customer company moves to another company or gets promoted, that may signal an opportunity to create a touch point, opening the door to work with them again.

New hires and job description postings: If an account you're interested in hires a new C-level or functional leader, you should consider this an opportunity to align with their new initiatives. New people nearly always signal change. Also if your company, competitor, product name, or any skills related to your business are included in a newly posted job description, that's worth investigating.

Funding rounds: A new influx of funding may mean expansion. This can be a good time to reach out.

Corporate news and announcements: When target accounts announce acquisitions, spin-offs, or even just that they had a great fiscal quarter, those signals become data points for you to activate on. Often companies announce their main initiatives and growth plans in public earnings calls. Not only can this indicate timing, it can help you with personalization touch points like we discussed in chapter 6.

Social media engagement: Likes, comments, interactions on Twitter, and LinkedIn posts are all worth noting. The job title, function, and nature of engagement all indicate where and how your message is resonating. If those indicators are on a competitor's content instead of your own, you have an additional layer of insight.

For several of these third-party intent signals, anyone across the marketing and sales teams can create alerts to track them without much overhead. Sign up for search engine emails that notify team members when target accounts appear in the news announcing newly secured funding or C-suite changes. Follow target accounts on social media and keep track of any publicly announced changes within the company. At Snowflake, we could pinpoint a potential upsell need by combining product telemetry data (which product workload a customer is using) with third-party research activity on a complementary workload. Shortly, we'll discuss how you can level up your company's use of intent data by consolidating signals and looking at trends, not just facts.

All of these signals can help in determining when you should target certain accounts. And some of these—such as campaign responses and job changes—can help you figure out whom to target first within those accounts.

That said, here's a crucial caveat: *Not all activity is meaningful!* It's easy to fall into the trap of believing that large numbers of clicks or high percentages are indicators of strong intent. This is only true when compared to the baseline. Say someone is tracking online activity and finds out that Snowflake has consumed online articles with terms related to "the data cloud" three hundred times per month. Sure, that's a lot, but Snowflake *is* the data cloud. Employees are likely performing those searches because they're part of their jobs and reflective of their day-to-day interest, not because they are in the market for a new cloud data platform. Third-party activity should be tracked as growth from the baseline. Has it changed? Increased? Look for *surges* in activity, since those are more likely to be meaningful.

Now you've got some data in hand about your target accounts. Your next step is to figure out what to do with it.

INSIDE THE IGLOO WITH SNOWFLAKE:

Guan Wang, global senior director of marketing intelligence at Snowflake, on how data science can help companies refine their timing

Guan leads the global and diverse Marketing Intelligence team at Snowflake to disrupt the aged B2B marketing analytics practices.

He is passionate about building high-performance teams to impact business results, driving growth strategy based on insights, as well as delivering best-in-class customer experience in the cloud computing industry. He has about fifteen years of revenue, strategy, operations, and analytics experience across the full customer life cycle (marketing, sales, and customer success) in high-growth startups and Fortune 500 companies. Guan holds undergraduate and graduate degrees in information systems and operations management, and completed accelerated training in data science and leadership development.

We asked him to speak about the basic inputs and tools that companies should consider when getting started with account scoring and prioritization.

> The first and easiest thing a company can do to start being more strategic about timing is just to track and rate engagement. You can do this by scoring your campaigns manually. Just create a spreadsheet, add the different types of campaigns you've been running, and assign a ranking based mostly on your intuition backed by any performance data you have. This isn't predictive, but it helps you track the types of campaigns that work best for you, and you can make timing decisions around that. To get started, make sure to include company size, revenue range, and recency of campaign engagement.
>
> If you want to try a third-party out-of-the-box model, you certainly can, but know that you'll be restricted by their models' preset inputs. The most complete and accurate way to create predictions is through a flexible and adaptable model custom-built for the needs of your business and data.
>
> To evaluate the reliability of a model, we use a measure called AUC or area under curve. AUC scores range between zero and one, and anything that rates at about 0.8 is pretty good.

Almost all of our machine-learning models at Snowflake get above 0.85 AUC score, which is extremely reliable, but we also have a lot of data and features to build from. For a startup or small company, if they tried to build a model with fewer features and could still get a 0.7 or 0.75 AUC score, that's relatively stable and worth working with. In my experience most third-party solutions get a 0.6, which is just slightly better than random guessing. So instead, I'd recommend that companies hire an agency or data science professionals to build some custom models for them.

Before we built out our current systems, we focused mostly on propensity scoring at Snowflake. On the marketing side we have the MQA, a marketing qualified account, which predicts the likelihood of opening up an opportunity on targeted accounts. And the second model is maturity scoring, which predicts how likely it is that an opportunity will be converted into a closed deal for sales. Both models share a lot of common features. They rely on account-level information like industry, where the company is headquartered, how many employees they have, and their revenue range, as well as first-party campaign engagement data from a variety of marketing channels. At Snowflake, we snapshot those features on a daily basis so we can compare them and take note of any changes in any of the categories. Changes influence the timing component of each account. This is a good place for companies to start if they really need to automate their timing decisions. An in-house business intelligence analyst, senior data analyst, or junior data scientist could create something like this.

The final level involves machine learning, which can be done at two levels. The prediction level uses a model or algorithms to summarize insights based on historic data. At the inference level you run data points into a machine learning model to calculate an output like a single numerical score. So for instance, we use the XGBoost algorithm—a supervised learning algorithm that tries to accurately predict a target variable by combining estimates from a set of simpler, weaker models—on new data coming in. It assigns values for every single feature, and that will give us a score. To use either of these to calculate account propensity and timing, you would need in-house data scientists who not only understand your product and customers very intimately, but also can automate prediction at scale with minimal human intervention.

Timing is complex, so whatever you can do to track and model behaviors will help you make better timing decisions.

How Do You Use Intent Data?

We strongly recommend keeping all of your intent data in one place. If it's spread across multiple databases or tools—or even people, who might be stashing it offline—no one will be able to see patterns in activity. This may be a customer relationship management (CRM) tool or a data cloud solution . . . even a spreadsheet can suffice in a pinch, as long as it's centralized and updated frequently.

If you have a CRM, you can create reports showing who is responding to your campaigns grouped by the account that they belong to. You can set up alerts in your marketing automation system showing people visiting your site from target accounts. In addition to filling and replenishing the data manually, you can make sure your CRM is keeping you abreast of emerging patterns that require attention. When those pop up, your teams can hop to and begin building campaigns against accounts for whom timing is clearly right.

When you're ready to level up from tracking intent data and reacting to it, your next step is to use it to build predictive models.

In addition to discussing intent in chapter 3 as an inspection metric, we touched on account propensity: the likelihood that an account will respond positively to sales outreach and eventually become a customer. Propensity scoring is a type of predictive modeling, and we view it as the gold standard for solving the timing challenge. It helps us to understand not only the volume of intent signals but also how meaningful they are to our goal of creating pipeline with sales. To determine propensity, we use predictive scoring models that employ machine learning and AI to pattern-match the intent signals that came from previously acquired customers at the time we sold to them. Then we use those patterns as a rubric to identify accounts showing similar indicators.

Moving from cumulative to predictive means moving from "What are the signals happening in target accounts?" to "What are the *patterns of intent signals* in our target accounts that have already shown up in previously acquired accounts?" You're going from monitoring the signals to understanding *what they mean.*

Predictive modeling is pretty complex, so most companies do one of three things to implement it: hire an agency to build it, buy an ABM platform that provides it, or build an in-house team of data scientists to create their own models.

At Snowflake we went for option three, and our data scientists have built one of the best predictive models in the business. And they did it natively in our own product. The sales-facing output is an action board (our version of a dashboard designed so users don't just look at it, but take action from it) called Arctic Insights that shows all accounts in an AE's territory. It delivers insights and topical intent data that capture all of the activity in the accounts owned by the viewer. We also created an MQA (Marketing Qualified Account) scoring threshold to indicate when the level of activity, combined with fit, indicates the best possible timing for sales outreach. We then paired that with an indicator of whether or not the

MQA account has been touched by sales in the last fourteen days to ensure no accounts get left behind. And with that, an action board is born.

While we are incredibly grateful to the Snowflake Marketing and Sales Intelligence teams (our data scientists), we know that some companies simply can't invest in predictive modeling at that level. That's OK. You can still amplify the impact of your one-team GTM efforts by starting out with one of the other options. Doing so will help you move beyond tracking and into insightful analysis.

Now let's dive into how timing and segmentation play off of one another. To do this, we'll need to revisit an example from chapter 4:

Let's say you work at a healthcare technology SAAS company with one thousand employees that is ready to expand beyond the single electronic health record system product component you launched with. You have researched your new buying personas for your billing product and know who your buying group includes and what technology you are displacing, as well as which size companies are large enough to feel the pain your product solves. You already know that your target industry is healthcare and that your ideal companies have 15,000 patient encounters per week or more, and you've created the following robust customer segments. This time, we have added additional bullet points for intent signals and relevant messages to each to show you how intent can further increase your impact in connecting with these accounts at the right time with the right message:

- **Hospital systems with more than four locations and fifteen thousand patient encounters/week/location**

Commonality: Disparate ER locations with high patient volume and disconnected billing

Relevant Intent Signals: Job postings for a meaningful increase in billing employees to handle the added work that disparate locations have created.

Relevant Message: Decrease your employee overhead with a centralized billing software.

Tip: Reference the job postings in your outreach from SDRs.

- **Clinic groups with more than six locations that have legacy billing software**

Commonality: Collaboration features that will save $500,000 a year in missed billing opportunities

Relevant Intent Signals: Third-party intent surges related to healthcare billing, your company, or competitor (especially legacy) alternatives that indicate their renewal is near.

Relevant Message: From the personalization you've done, you know which vendor they currently use. Reference three points of value they can expect by switching to your product.

Tip: *Never* mention that you saw an increase in web behavior, which comes off as creepy. Let the nature of timing and relevance work for themselves.

- **Healthcare providers in a specific state that rolled out new compliance regulations for billing practices**

Commonality: Need to migrate technologies to maintain compliance under new regulations

Relevant Intent Signals: The nature of the segment itself *is* an intent signal. The fact that the target accounts must deal with compliance regulations by a specific date creates timing and intent on its own.

Relevant Message: This type of requirement adds working hours and stress. Draw on your persona learnings from chapter 5 and focus on how you can help with the change's personal downstream impact.

Tip: Provide a resource library that they can continually reference as their "go-to" source of information for the compliance regulation.

You've got a sense of the importance of timing in ABM motions and are starting to get some systems in place to track it and act upon it, but what about those must-win accounts? You can't wait for them to signal readiness in the same ways these target accounts do. But you can use timing to find creative ways to capture their attention.

Leveraging Timing in Must-Win Accounts

For those accounts you *must* pursue, you can still leverage timing to make your approaches more effective. Whether it is prioritizing a specific line of business because one of your prior customer advocates took on a new role in it, or intent keywords led you to believe that a surging topic relates to a specific department, each signal becomes a clue along the treasure hunt. Though you may have to hunt multiple times and with multiple strategies before you strike gold.

Hillary describes this as the robot vacuum approach to one-team GTM. When you turn on your robot vacuum, it starts its little vacuuming rounds, and sometimes it hits a wall. But instead of just stopping and giving up on vacuuming altogether, the machine simply switches directions and tries again until it finds an open space that needs to be relieved of dust bunnies. With must-win accounts, you're likely to hit some walls, but being persistent pays off.

Must-win accounts frequently exist as part of industry lists like the Fortune 2000 and have multiple subsidiaries, arms, or business units. At Snowflake, we've used the strategy of tracking intent signals related to individual subsidiaries and acting on those to identify which door in the hallway is most likely to be open for the robot vacuum to enter first. If we can find an in with a single subsidiary, that lays the groundwork for finding customers in others over time.

Intent signals like job changes are fantastic for must-win accounts. If a new CIO was hired within a particular subsidiary, prioritize reaching out to that subsidiary over any others for the time being. Take this opportunity to get to know your persona inside and out, and send them a welcome box in their new role. Funding rounds can also be helpful, as can announcements of acquisitions and spin-offs. Celebrating these alongside your target accounts shows your allyship and establishes you as a supportive partner before ever doing business together.

If you have a must-win account that's offering *no* intent signals, it makes the burden to provide value that much greater. The Problem Education work you do becomes paramount so you can prove that your offering will improve the company's product, standing, or revenue opportunities. With no signals, you're trying to compel action and make your own timing.

Now you've got the lay of the timing land. Let's look at a type of play you can run that hinges on issues of timing.

Example Play Centered on Timing

Timing should be a consideration in all of your planned account-based plays, but there are a handful of instances where timing is the primary consideration. Here's an example:

One of our favorite plays is something we created after seeing the initial success of the travel company win we mentioned at the start of this chapter. In order to scale the success of that program, we created a timing-based play called "Arctic Accelerator."

We monitor all accounts owned by sales and if they surge at an extra-high score—like in the top 5 to 10 percent of the scoring range—we pull them out based on sales' approval and target them with ABM, SDR, and sales touch points. We do this on a weekly basis in some regions, which accomplishes two things:

It creates a weekly topic of conversation to reinforce the alignment between your cross-functional teams. Reviewing the surging accounts, identifying messaging, and activating together is a muscle that needs to be strengthened, and this is the perfect conditioning exercise.

It builds trust between marketing and sales, because marketing is surfacing actionable insights that deliver results very quickly. So much so that we recommend this play for individuals who are reluctant to adopt an account-based approach. The results are fast, and the lift is light.

Service-Level Agreements Tie in to Timing

Timing needs to be monitored internally, too, among the ABM team, SDRs, and most members of sales and marketing. If the timing is right within an account but your own internal team members don't act quickly enough, the window of opportunity may close. Most companies know that inbound leads need to be dealt with in a set time frame, but so do outbound accounts! And if your teams don't agree on time frames for action, your best intent-data efforts may be for naught.

At Snowflake, we require documented commitments from SDRs and sales that they are in agreement with the play and will follow up on intent signals in a timely manner. If an account does X, sales and SDRs need to respond within Y amount of time, or they'll lose out on an important opportunity. We have streams of data coming in from engagements, and more data going out from different touch points, and our Arctic Insights dashboard compiles all of it to show what has been followed up on and what hasn't been followed up on.

Tyrus Abram, Snowflake's senior director of sales development, is a big fan of service-level agreements (SLAs) and the cohesion they create. He told us, "During my first six months at Snowflake, it felt a bit like organized chaos. We didn't have any service level agreements in place between sales and marketing, so we had no way to prioritize the inbound leads or outbound accounts. We were just hitting everything with the same behavior, hitting every-thing with the same level of priority, which was a huge mistake since not all accounts are created equal. We needed to sort out what needed to be responded to in seventy-two hours versus forty-eight or twenty-four hours. So getting that off the ground was imperative."

SLAs like ours may seem nitpicky, but they have helped us achieve a one-team GTM strategy. They unlock the ability to get people accountable and keep them aligned. They are a silo-busting tool that builds trust and enables all teams to collaborate more effi-ciently and smoothly. As you scale your own account-based efforts, consider adding some SLAs to the mix so timing remains top-of-mind for everyone.

ACTION + OWNER	COMMUNICATION	NOTES
ABM MANAGER Identify a broad list of ABM-eligible accounts that can be pulled from to create programs later.	Email documents to review 48 hrs before call ABM/DM/SDR 1:1 to communicate need and review - AE returns final list within 48 hours	Start with all named accounts and ask for DMs to remove any they do not want you working *This exercise should be done at start of Q1 and Q3 to maintain alignment
SDR MANAGER Enable SDR team with refreshing/training session on topic selected	SDR Manager review basecamp basics with team to enable selling motion- 3 main points, elevator pitch and decks available	ABM will share topic and SDR manager set up for second Wednesday of the quarter This is the time for the SDR manager to also review the sequence that will be used with the team and highlight functional actions
ABM MANAGER Identify priority themes/topics for DM within their region to begin account selection	ABM/SDR/DM Kickoff call	RVP priorities should be documented at the start of each quarter to ensure DM nominations align ABM brings surging topics to meeting to discuss
ABM MANAGER Provide list of surging accounts within identified topic(s) for review	Email to AEs, DMs and SDRs with list of accounts Follow up email 48 hours later	Use Arctic Insights to identify accounts, include intent scores, CMQA, or others requested by sales Prioritize suspect accounts with last SDR activity > 90 days. Must be greenfield unless mini majors.

Here's a chart from an internal Snowflake document showing how we hold each other accountable through SLAs. Yours may look different, but take this step across all actions for all programs. Without it, it will be impossible to enforce accountability.

Now you know that intent data tells you, in great detail, who is looking for what and *when*. It allows you to present your messages at the right time, show them to people precisely when they're most relevant, and develop the right message to get you closer to closing important accounts.

In chapter 8, we'll give you some example plays so you can begin the process of planning your own programs, using intent data and timing to guide you.

MINIMUM VIABLE PARAMETERS
Collect, analyze, and activate on first-party intent signals.

SCALED PARAMETERS
Find a way to combine first- and third-party intent signals into a predictive model or score.

MISTAKES TO AVOID
Don't forget that some activity isn't meaningful!

Don't ignore what the intent data says, use it in your messaging.

Don't assume other teams know what to do when intent signals happen.

8

Plan Your First Plays

The unified outbound motion at Snowflake is referenced as a best-in-class GTM motion. However, to be fully transparent, it hasn't always run smoothly. The journey of learning, making each other the best, and constantly improving continues even as you read this book. But one of our biggest learning moments came early on, as we were trying to plan our plays as one GTM team.

At that time, we had the illusion of alignment—of who was responsible for what—and set out to run a one-to-many play with all the "ready, set, go!" gusto of a team who had it figured out. But we found out the hard way that our teams really did not know what they were responsible for or when they should take action. Specifically, we did not see the expected lift in SDR meetings compared to our "cold outbound" historical baseline and knew something was off.

What did we do to diagnose the problem? We looked at our inspection metrics to find out what was going wrong. Immediately, we saw that people weren't being added correctly into our SDR sequences. So we asked SDRs why not and were told that SDRs themselves were never told which specific sequence to use for the campaign, so they were going rogue with what they believed was good messaging. Then we talked with the SDR managers and asked why there was so much confusion among their direct reports. It turns out that the managers assumed the ABM team had run the enablement. Despite our best intentions, we had chaos. It became painfully clear that more prescription in roles and responsibilities was a must.

Planning our plays wasn't enough. We needed to create a comprehensive, tactical playbook that everyone across marketing and sales, including ABMers and SDRs, could consult whenever they had questions.

We did that. We made a big, detailed playbook that captured roles, meeting cadence, deliverables, and time lines from the moment a play should be initiated to the time it wrapped up. It's helped a lot, and we strongly recommend you do the same. Codifying our plays had a measurable impact on our success rate: We went from booking a meeting with one in every thirteen accounts we targeted to one in every three accounts we targeted.

But we still have hiccups now and again, because, frankly, One-Team GTM is incredibly complex. And when you have multiple teams not just trying to plan together but also trying to turn the knobs and flip the switches and *execute* together, that takes ongoing coordination. You need to be super prescriptive and define the obvious, while also being willing to course-correct if making a procedural change becomes necessary.

We share this because you're probably going to implement some of what we recommend and hit some snags of your own. That doesn't mean your program failed or that you should give up. It just means that you're working through a complex process while simultaneously trying to bust through some long-standing internal silos. It's a lot to take on. If things go sideways, retrace your steps. Check your inspection metrics, look back through some previous chapters in this book, find out what needs adjustment, and try again.

In fact, we hope you will revisit this chapter *and* the previous ones again and again. Partially because we know you'll need to tweak and refine your own one-team GTM processes, but also because many of the steps we're outlining here may be done sooner or later than we recommend. Many can be executed simultaneously. As you read through this book, know that everything we're presenting is meant to be flexible. Adapt it all to suit your company's unique needs, and always be willing to make adjustments if a strategy stops working.

But when this alignment does come together, the plays you execute will transform the way you impact your revenue goals as one team.

What Is a Play and How Do You Build One?

The silo busting, system calibrating, and content stockpiling you've done before now is about to pay off. The segments you've defined and personas you've built are ready to meet up with your content libraries, because one-team "plays" are all about bringing those assets together and activating them. As we explored in chapter 6, this is comparable to working through a classic jigsaw puzzle. Before you make a plan to send emails or make any landing pages go live, you've got to:

Take Inventory: Sort your puzzle pieces so you know what you are working with. (Which you've done by sorting and categorizing the content in your library.)

Gather Intel: Figure out which picture you are building so you know what "good" looks like. (Which you've done by segmenting the market, creating robust personas, and determining which metrics merit tracking.)

Only after you've tackled those can you begin to:

Build Experiences: Assemble the puzzle. We use the term "experience" to capture the end-to-end touch points a prospect or customer will receive. They can span across digital, physical, events, etc.

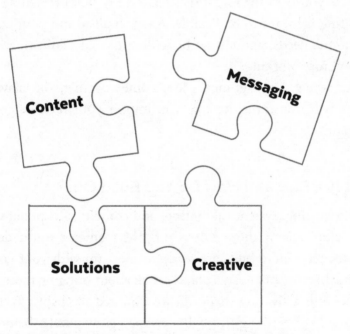

Think about personalization like completing a puzzle.

The "experiences" you build are born from your plays. And those plays will draw upon the tech solutions, messaging, creative assets, and content you have at your disposal. They're the activity that unifies all the strategic work that marketing and sales have been doing together. They're the puzzle assembled to completion.

What is a play? A defined series of tactics executed between ABM, SDRs, and sales to drive a specific outcome within a target account.

What are the components of a play?

Who you're talking to (personas)

What you're telling them (message)

How you will communicate the message (content)

How you will deliver the message (SDR Plays, marketing channels)

What's a formula for creating a play?
Plays can take many different forms, so we've got more of a rubric than a formula for you. Whether you adopt this rubric or create your own, we do recommend creating a repeatable, scalable process for planning plays that all teams can reference and agree upon. Doing that is critical to the success of your ABM program. The following components and time line are a great place to start:

Establish Baseline Metrics and Program Goals: Identify SDR and marketing baseline metrics and program targets. Examples include: Account engagement rate with marketing, contacts sequenced, SDR response rate, account to booked/completed meetings rate.

Identify Roles and Responsibilities: Depending on your account mix, you may want sales, SDRs, and ABM to play different roles to achieve your desired outcome outlined above. Identify who is responsible for what, in what time frame.

Calendar Reminders: Place calendar reminders for each of the following steps on a shared calendar with all parties involved for each quarter moving forward.

Select Accounts: Use data to choose the most-ripe accounts for your effort. Refresh the accounts included in your TAM at least on an annual basis. Select the specific cohort of accounts to activate four weeks ahead of SDR launch. (More on activation in chapter 9.)

Complete Targeting and Messaging Matrices: Associate personas, products, messaging, and intent keywords with baseline outreach sequences for seamless execution.

Work on Program Development: Develop messaging, choose content, build experience touch points, and enrich contacts in accounts if needed three weeks before SDR launch.

Launch Advertising: Launch marketing activities to selected accounts with identified 1:1 or 1:Few ads 2 weeks prior to SDR launch.

Launch SDR Prospecting: Kick off sequence using recommended throttling and personalization at start of quarter or agreed upon date.

Optimize: Measure sequenced contacts, response rate, booked/completed meetings, and opportunities weekly. Adjust for optimization.

Many of these steps will look familiar to you, but the calendar reminders are new. And we want to take a moment to emphasize how ridiculously simple and vitally important they are. The hard truth is this: If you assume everyone on your teams knows what they should be doing and when, you're wrong. We implemented calendar reminders as shared, highly visible guidance for when each stakeholder needed to do each task. They created transparency and virtually eliminated the phrase "I didn't know" from team member vocabularies. From a leadership perspective, calendar reminders enable accountability since everything is documented. This has been a critical step for success that was implemented after our "family meeting" to what was not working.

The other steps in this rubric help you align cooperation between teams, creation of content, distribution of content, and the crucial and often-overlooked step of reviewing your work and optimizing your processes using what you've learned. If you make your own rubric, please promise us you'll include a review and optimization step at the end.

Because you need to ensure your processes are working, and the only way to do that is to measure, analyze, and tweak. If no one is reading what you're writing or seeing what you're creating, *you need to know about that* so you can make changes to your strategies. Content is only content if you can get it in front of the people who need to see it. Without strategic delivery, it's just assets. So as you begin planning plays, you'll need to build in some ways to review and revise your processes.

	Week -4	Week -3	Week -2	Week -1	Week 0	Week 1	Week 2	Week 3	Week 4	Week 5	Week 6	Week 7	Week 8

Q Start

PLANNING
- X Sync
- Account Plans

ABM
- Value Selling Doc
- DB Enrichment
- Target Ads + ABM Page
- Event Promotions

SALES
- Outbound to VP+

Sales needs to be driving insights and collaboration

SDR
- Sequence Dev
- Outbound + Event Promos
- Event Follow Up

FM
- Event

- Start Next Cycle

Example of a calendar of collaboration

INSIDE THE IGLOO WITH SNOWFLAKE:

Tyrus Abram, senior director of sales development at Snowflake, on refining account knowledge and building plays

Tyrus has been in SaaS/Tech sales for thirteen years after starting as an SDR, and spending half that time as an AE before leading teams at both pre- and post-IPO companies. His last four-plus years have been at Snowflake, building the sales development org, and he currently leads the US Verticals team as a senior director. He loves basketball and has a passion for building go-to-market teams and developing young sales professionals.

We asked him to speak about his experience joining Snowflake and watching the ABM/SDR partnership evolve from enthusiastic but scattered efforts to strategic, coordinated motions complete with thoughtful plays.

When I first started at Snowflake, we had maybe four people at the company with ABM in their title. And what they were able to help us do was identify and prioritize all of the accounts that we should care about as an organization. Instead of trying to boil the ocean, we focused on about six thousand accounts that made up our TAM. So that was a good first step. But even still, the SDRs were just going after the accounts that were put in front of them.

Cross-functional plays started to evolve and mature when Hillary came on board and the ABM group started to grow. Now we're able to say, "This is a play that should last ten months," or "This is a play that should last two years ongoing," "This is a one-quarter play," "This is a one-month play." And we can also specify, "This is what needs to be said by the SDR if we're going after CMOs within the retail space." Now we're literally putting together Gantt charts of when the ABM team should be reaching out, what information they should share, when direct mail should be sent out, and when they should be hit with personalized ads specific to their persona.

Figuring all that out took a lot of trial and error and a lot of AB testing and a lot of failure alongside the success. But I think it comes back to really knowing your target account, knowing your market, knowing your personas, and approaching them at the right time.

Learning about your target accounts is done by tracking when people are searching our website, along with our competitors, so we can see what they care about when. We can see who within their team could benefit from talking to us and about what particular workload. I think that's something that any company can invest in. They can start to identify with their own current customer base— even if they've only sold to five or ten customers—who they should be selling to and within which industries. Who you should go after and why is something that can be codified. All companies can start to do that today, regardless of what they sell and who they sell to.

Example One-Team GTM plays

In chapter 4 we talked about the various ways to divide up one-team GTM execution: one-to-one, one-to-few, and one-to-many. That segmentation becomes highly relevant again now as you strategize your first plays. The tactics and investments you deploy for a one-to-one play will be different from those that work for a one-to-few or one-to-many play.

One-to-One Plays

This approach is reserved for must-win accounts, or "needle-movers" as our GVP of Enterprise Sales likes to call them. We find that the accounts best suited for this program are those that include more than ten subsidiaries, have some sort of momentum with our business already in play, and yet have at least 80 percent of the account still unpenetrated. The goal then becomes to use the relationships we have in place to grow our footprint in the account.

One-to-one play as door opener: We recommend reserving a one-to-one approach for new opportunity accounts where the account has unique traits like a nontraditional buying cycle, political tension, or very high spending potential. This approach can also be used when a one-to-many approach has not been successful. At Snowflake, we reserve it for must-win accounts identified by sales. In our consulting experience, these have been also used to win a company's first landmark account. Basically, this is a resource-intensive play and your target customers need to be worth it. The size and involvement of the play can vary widely in size, breadth, depth, and investment based on your resources and account priority.

Who you're talking to (personas): Start by identifying which buying group within the account is best suited for an opportunity, then identify paths of entry to that group. You may have an existing relationship you want to leverage, know someone who can make an introduction, have a partner well-situated in the account, or want to start with the end user who may become your champion. If you are lost as to where to start, consider using a third-party vendor to provide account mapping to you for additional insights. It's worth the time to discuss the strategy for each of these accounts in detail with your GTM team.

What you're telling them (message): This is the first conversation you are having in the account, so you will need to establish who you are and why they should care. (Focus on Problem Education from chapter 6). Tailor this message to the individuals you identified in the prior step.

How you will communicate the message (content): 1:1 door-opener campaigns need to provide a well-curated library of content for the prospect to anonymously engage with as they learn about the problem and viable solutions. Make sure to include content that relates to any partners they work with, tech they currently leverage, and thought leadership you can provide. If compelling, this content will get forwarded and shared around the business by the contacts you targeted directly. You can continue to update this as you receive analytics that show which pieces of content are and are not getting engagement.

How you will deliver the message (SDR/sales plays, marketing channels): Touch points should include digital advertising tailored and targeted to the personas you have identified and pointing to both your content library and early-stage offers like webinars or short-form content like blogs and e-books. SDR outreach should be to senior director level and below, AE outreach to VP level and above, and the opportunity to book an initial conversation should be prevalent just about anywhere this account lands. We also encourage you to have SDRs engage with the prospects' content on social media as well as invite them to relevant events by industry, solution, or territory.

Timing: You can use just about any intent signal for one-to-one, but we recommend timing this based on which accounts are the absolute must-win for your sales leadership teams. (This means timing could be irrelevant if you need to pursue them regardless.) We also recommend reserving these for sales' top two to five accounts, and launching them at quarter-start to align with their prospecting efforts.

Goals: The ultimate goal is to get a first meeting in your high-priority account. Inspection metrics you can look at along the way include anonymous engagement (page visits, social media post reactions, review site visits) and known engagement (campaign responders, email replies, and comments on social media posts).

One-to-One Play as Opportunity Accelerator: We find the one-to-one approach to be most successful for accounts that have open opportunities. This is particularly important for accounts with robust buying committees, known to take many layers of approvals with lengthy contract reviews.

Who you're talking to (personas): The personas you target will vary throughout the duration of the play depending on the milestone. For example, when you first kick off, target the entire buying committee. When contract review starts, target the CFO and finance teams. Then when security review begins, target the security and IT teams. By the end, you will have a multi-threaded campaign targeting the entire buying committee.

What you're telling them (message): Your message needs to be specific to the buying committee cohorts you are targeting. To continue the example from above, the messaging for the finance teams should touch on how you will save the company money, while the message to the security team should touch on how you mitigate risk for the company.

How you will communicate the message (content): The content library becomes more robust for this type of play, often presented as a microsite with different tabs of content and offers per buying committee member. You have the option of keeping this outward and marketing-focused, or using it to upload call recordings and relevant decks that the team can leverage as they go through your buying process. If you do the latter, ensure you have proper security in place to limit access to just the people at your prospect account.

How you will deliver the message (SDR/sales plays, marketing channels): Marketing should tread lightly during this phase, being sure to respect the direction of the account owner. Light digital touch points for brand awareness, tailored to each persona, are best. On the SDR side, you similarly want to present a coherent and united front to the account. Avoid appearing disjointed by executing "tag-team" outreach between the SDR and the AE. This can range from simply copying the AE on email outreach to dovetailing AE emails into the same communication threads that SDRs initiate.

Timing: Once an opportunity has been opened, initiate your first campaign. Consider additional timing milestones like sales conversations with new buying committee members, the start of contract negotiations, and security reviews as additional timing elements to refresh your campaign with content tailored to the respective audiences for those milestones.

Goals: Your KPI for this play should be the number of days from the time the opportunity was open to the time it was won, compared to the average time-to-close for accounts of similar deal size. That said, make sure you have a suite of inspection metrics to consider as well. We find that accounts large enough to deserve this treatment often naturally have slower cycles, or that ABM is brought in because the deal is stuck, skewing your KPI metrics. Looking at other indicators like deal size and anecdotal feedback from the selling teams and buying teams on their experience during the process to provide an added layer of insight on your success.

Final note: The benefit of 1:1 is that you can really customize it for any buying stage, buying group, individual, or combination of factors. We will touch on how to use 1:1 as an expansion play for existing customers in chapter 12.

One-to-Few Plays

You can activate one-to-few for a variety of needs, but we've mainly used it to address various segments simultaneously who have tech-stack nuances unique to bigger cohorts. Using one-to-few allows us to accommodate those nuances at the segment level while leveraging the scaled infrastructure of one-to-many.

One-to-Few Play #1: Feature Adoption: We recommend this play for engaging high-value accounts that are either current customers, or using a trial/freemium version of your product. It also works best when your product serves multiple distinct use cases or user groups. Ultimately the goal is to position the value of another product feature or encourage the account to adopt an upgraded version of your product.

Who you're talking to (personas): The personas you will target depend on the type of feature set and use case that's currently in use at the target account. For example, if you sell a quoting solution that's been adopted by the sales organization but has accounting features available to accountants, you would target this play at the finance persona. You can also target current champions within the account: Who have you delighted to the point where they will make an introduction on your behalf?

What you're telling them (message): This is where product telemetry—how end users are engaging with your product—becomes a powerful resource. If sales and marketing have a clear picture of which SKUs or product features are *not* being used by an account, then ABM, SDRs, and sales can collectively identify ways to drive feature adoption. Messaging should focus on the incremental pain solved by those underused features and/or the cost savings of consolidating technologies. Show them you know them by sharing current adoption insights, but don't alienate your customer with an invasive level of detail about what they're doing in your product.

How you will communicate the message (content): The microsite becomes even more powerful in a one-to-few strategy as you can scale out relevance to even more accounts. Focus the microsite on education for a specific product feature that's not being used by the segment of accounts you are targeting. Include tailored demos that walk the audience through exactly how you solve any challenges you assume they have. Consider positioning offers such as limited-time feature access, hands-on learning sessions, and paid pilots that offer immediate value. Your sales and sales engineering teams, as well as professional services, become important players in this approach since they have the most depth of knowledge about the customer's current usage strategy and landscape. The ultimate goal of the content you create is to feed their touch points.

How you will deliver the message (SDR/sales plays, marketing channels): If your product has a user interface, work with the product team to implement light in-app call-to-actions. Physical events are also a powerful lever for this kind of one-to-few play, providing the opportunity for customers who have already adopted the feature to influence target accounts who have not yet made the switch. SDRs should work closely with AEs on account-based messaging and securing referrals in a way that does not harm the existing customer relationship. If there is a specific technology or consulting partner that specializes in this feature's adoption, consider doing joint-marketing efforts with them across the above activations.

Timing: Look for longer-term buildup of intent signals for keywords related to a specific feature. This intent should be evaluated on a quarterly or monthly basis and reviewed with sales counterparts to weed out any accounts that may be false positives. If you can measure freemium feature engagement with your product, that can provide another timing event depending on the breadth and depth of that engagement. You can also monitor third-party technology data to understand if your target accounts have recently started using a competitive solution for the feature you are promoting, and use that as a campaign trigger.

Goals: For freemium/trial accounts, focus on conversion to opportunity for longer sales cycles or conversion to paid usage for shorter sales cycles. For increasing adoption with existing customers, measure creation of opportunities related to the new SKU or use case. Feature adoption directly within the product provides another goalpost for success.

One-to-Few Play #2: Competitive Takeout: This play is all about identifying accounts with a competitive install base and launching a pinpoint attack focused on the soft spot in that vendor's solution. It's a perfect fit for the balanced focus and breadth of one-to-few.

Who you're talking to (personas): Make persona targeting decisions very carefully for this play. There are almost always individuals within a company who have made big, visible career decisions on purchasing and implementing the solution you are now attempting to take out. Identify these people through sources like LinkedIn and avoid engaging them directly. Instead look for new hires in decision-making roles, especially those who moved over from another existing customer.

What you're telling them (message): The thrust of your message should highlight success stories of similar customers who've migrated from this competitor over to your camp. Focus on the "why" and "why now" of those stories. Don't over-rotate on talking about how this company might use your competitor. Rather, jump right to assumed gaps that only your solution can fill.

How you will communicate the message (content): Create messaging that fits between Solution Research and Solution Selection. If you know that all of the accounts being targeted are already familiar with you (perhaps you previously lost opportunities at those accounts), then curate content that challenges the status quo or focuses on innovative strategies that the incumbent can't support. Feature videos and testimonials from current customers discussing the headaches of the "old way" of your competitor. Offer highly consultative sessions with an industry expert who can provide a road map that your solution is uniquely suited to deliver upon.

How you will deliver the message (SDR/sales plays, marketing channels): If you get the timing and message right for accounts in this play, then it's all-systems-go with the sales and marketing channels you have at your disposal. Run retargeting ads at new hires. Get SDRs on the phone with low-level end users to gather information on the weak points of your competition. Run customer office-hour webinars discussing the road map to migrating onto your solution. Have AEs build competitive pitch decks showing where the competition is likely coming up short. Send account-based emails with tailored invitations to a local meet-and-greet and engage these accounts in places you know they will already be, like industry events, community groups, and online forums.

Timing: You could choose to launch a competitive takeout play at any time depending on the priorities of the business such as taking a new innovation to market that gives your solution an edge in feature parity. However, the gold standard for timing competitive takeouts is striking just when your competitor's contracts are up for renewal. If SDRs have sleuthed out these dates from their prior outreach and logged them in your CRM, you can launch this play just as the account is open to alternative solutions. New executive hires or decision-makers joining the company also open the door to rip-and-replace conversations.

Goals: Ultimately you are moving accounts either from the target stage to the engaged stage or the working stage to the meeting stage. Set up targets based on the number of accounts moved between stages and keep an eye on inspection metrics like content consumption and contacts worked per account.

While one-to-few can make an impact on its own, it can also be powerful as an add-on to a one-to-one campaign for a blended approach. For example, if you are targeting a large, Fortune 500 account with high-level messaging across the business, you may want to engage two or three subsidiaries in parallel with a one-to-few message specific to those subsidiaries and their pain points. In many of these conglomerates, the subsidiaries span multiple industries, so bespoke messaging for each is helpful.

One-to-Many Plays

These plays are intended to identify accounts with active buying interest in specific topics in each region, and then secure a first meeting with them at scale. We've found that the best way to run these plays is to focus on a specific topic or industry; either connect with sales and let them select the topic, or ask the ABM team to identify a topic by running buying intent reports. In either case, start with a list of fifty to two hundred accounts that are showing buying intent on a common topic, then target them as a cohort with consistent messaging, content, etc.

One-to-Many Play #1: Warm Calling: This approach is systematic in nature and all about timing for a one-two punch. Each quarter, you will kick off a set of cross-functional activities prior to quarter end, effectively warming up accounts before sales and SDRs activate on the same accounts with the same message at quarter start. We call this warm calling because a top-performing SDR responded after using this play by telling us he "no longer did cold calling." Thanks to ABM, his accounts were already familiar with the company and the value message, and we coined the term "warm calling."

Who you're talking to (personas): Because this is a scaled play, we recommend creating cohorts by district or territory. This allows you to tailor campaign elements to the audience that each sales district needs to prioritize, while still benefiting from a scaled approach. Once each district chooses their cohort (e.g., technology leaders in manufacturing in territory 1 and business admins in retail in territory 2), you will need to identify the coordinating titles and personas for each cohort.

What you're telling them (message): You need to ensure that knowledge sharing happens with each district in order to nail down a message unique to each. You may be focusing on problem education in territory 1, while you may be doing an upsell motion in territory 2. Having program templates in place will help you standardize the outputs for each category. Consider a template to be a consistent format you can request input in, create messaging and copy, and delineate touch points.

How you will communicate the message (content): Each cohort by territory will get its own content hub/microsite with coordinating advertising copy and SDR sequences. The type and volume of content will vary depending on your persona and buying stage.

How you will deliver the message (SDR/sales plays, marketing channels): This play works best as a simplistic approach; otherwise scale becomes too complex. ABM targets accounts using digital advertising across multiple channels two to four weeks before the SDRs activate sequences pointing to the same content with the same message to the same people. Typically, AEs are most involved in the account selection and account intelligence, then come back once an SDR has met with and qualified the responders.

Timing: Timing is everything here. This play works best when you use third-party web intent as the primary qualifier for account selection. It can work two ways: Sales teams can request a topic and marketing can provide a list of accounts surging on that topic, or marketing can provide a list of topics surging, and sales can pick which one they want to use. In one instance, we had a single territory choose *not* to use intent for timing, and instead pick their own topic based on instinct. The other regions saw four times the results of the one that went on instinct. Needless to say, they all use timing now.

Goals: We are strictly focused on SDR meetings as the primary KPI. Secondary KPIs or inspection metrics to watch are engaged accounts (are the targeted accounts even engaging with marketing, and therefore "warm," for the warm calling effort?), and opportunity rate (as you increase the meeting booking effectiveness, is quality suffering? Or are they converting to opportunities at an equal or even higher rate than they would *without* warm calling?).

One-to-Many Play #2: EOQ Push: Want to make quota-carrying teams your best friends? Analyze the specific teams and regions who are at risk of missing their quotas for the quarter and offer up this one-to-many play to get things back on track.

Who you're talking to (personas): We've focused on account segmentation throughout this book, but this play is all about segmenting individuals within those accounts. Specifically, target the contacts who are active in sequences for the sales and SDR teams but have not yet responded to the outreach. Think of this as a "play within a play." Salespeople at your company are already working these contacts for one reason or another, and now you're injecting a boost of awareness on top of that outreach. Most sales engagement platforms offer a CRM integration to flag contacts who are active in a sequence and which sequence they're engaging with. At minimum, you can segment based on the contact status and make an educated guess on messaging based on their persona or industry.

What you're telling them (message): Your colleagues have already developed a "hypothesis of need" and messaging strategy for the contacts that they are reaching out to. Take the subject matter of those sequences and translate them into additional use cases, customer stories, and value propositions. Sync directly with the sales teams to align on messaging if necessary.

How you will communicate the message (content): Dig back into your content library for the highest-performing offers that are quick to spin up and deploy. Persona-based advertisements and existing microsites focused on industry use cases work really well here, but you want to make sure that a conversion point is available for the individual to transition from anonymous to known engagement, triggering the service-level agreement process. It's also an opportunity to get creative and scrappy. Maybe you have excess inventory from a previous swag campaign or some extra budget to sweeten the call to action that your SDRs are offering.

How you will deliver the message (SDR/sales plays, marketing channels): Run retargeted ads for the sequenced contacts to position your offer, using their email addresses rather than audience traits for targeting. Consider one-off emails that SDRs and AEs can send out in addition to their sequenced messages with the new content. For example, we targeted contacts with a "book club in a box" paid social ad that offered a physical copy of Frank Slootman's *Rise of the Data Cloud* along with a reader's guide and coffee mug. Contacts who had ignored the SDR could now engage with the offer, which was fed back to that SDR and opened a new opportunity to engage.

Timing: Think about this play around the midpoint of the fiscal quarter. Run reports and meet with sales teams to identify which teams have the greatest risk of missing their quarterly number. Mobilize resources to activate the play with at least a month left before the quarter closes.

Goals: If you're helping SDRs get to quota, measure movement of accounts from working status to meeting status. If you're helping AEs get to quota, measure movement of accounts from opportunity status to closed won status.

In addition to one-to-many plays, you can apply this methodology more broadly for what we call targeted demand gen. In past roles, we have created an always-on strategy where timing triggers are identified by intent spikes in specific topics; accounts are distributed into topic and journey-stage segments accordingly; and marketing activations subsequently kick off.

For example, you could have three segments per solution, one for each stage of the buying cycle. As accounts meet the thresholds you set, they begin receiving digital touch points with messaging related to the topic they surged in, including a three-step email nurture. As the accounts engage with the content you provide, you can push them to subsequent stages, with coordinating messaging and touch points more specific to the next stage, like booking a demo or attending an event. This approach requires a bit of creativity in how you string together your tech stack, but with a scrappy mindset and a little innovation, you will be on your way.

Don't Be Afraid to Dive In

The key to making your plays work is to *actually execute them*. For far too many companies, account-based becomes the brilliant strategy that sits on the shelf. Don't let that happen to you. Embrace a bias toward action and start running a pilot.

All you need to do this is yourself and one other person: someone from marketing and someone from sales. Who is most open to working together in one of the sales or marketing groups? Who is close to the customer, and may be eager to find ways to serve that customer better? Seek out that person and plan a small, cheap, fast, low-risk pilot together. Begin with something you know you can win. One segment, one program, one customer.

We gave you a perfect example of a pilot program back in chapter 1: Hillary's team was running targeted advertisements on LinkedIn, and they were generating interest in Snowflake's offerings, but no one had direct follow-through planned. Travis suggested they work together on a quick play that the sales development representatives (SDRs) could execute: reaching out to people who had clicked on, commented on, or liked the ads, and following up with them. Within two weeks, we were booking meetings for sales from those ad engagements. Remember, compel action by understanding what success looks like to your partners in the business. Travis knew that Hillary's team needed to show results in the form of meetings, and this play was a shortcut to that.

Go ahead and adopt this play from us, try it out with one marketing person and one salesperson, record your results, and start building from there. Believe us when we say that getting those first few plays up and running is . . . well, thrilling. They work quickly and yield amazing results, which means you and your partner are likely to feel encouraged and excited by this new way of working. Keep that momentum going.

But also remember that whatever you do now in this experimental phase can be easily undone.

Although we feel confident that you can stand up an account-based practice in most companies, we also know that doing so is fairly low-risk. If it doesn't work, you stop doing it. This is what Amazon founder Jeff Bezos terms a "two-way door."

Some decisions are consequential and irreversible or nearly irre-versible—one-way doors—and these decisions must be made methodically, carefully, slowly, with great deliberation and con-sultation. If you walk through and don't like what you see on the other side, you can't get back to where you were before. We can call these Type 1 decisions.

But most decisions aren't like that—they are changeable, reversible—they're two-way doors. If you've made a sub-optimal Type 2 decision, you don't have to live with the consequences for that long. You can reopen the door and go back through. Type 2 decisions can and should be made quickly by high judgment individuals or small groups.[1]

Given that running a few simple, data-driven, one-team plays puts your company at extremely low risk of catastrophe, we urge you to give it a try. Don't exhaust yourself making a huge library of content first or get mired in indecision; try something! And then keep exper-imenting, measuring, and learning from your results. Let yourself fail fast, pivot, and adjust. Then recalibrate and keep iterating until you've got a practice you can scale.

And as you do that, continue to build alignment and work toward busting those silos. The reason Snowflake has become so successful with a one-team GTM approach is because we've defined roles, codified processes, and created lasting alignment.

We've also mastered the art of timing our plays, a topic we'll explore in the coming chapter.

---

1   Bezos, Jeffrey. "1998 Shareholder Letter." Amazon. https://www.sec.gov/
    Archives/edgar/data/1018724/000119312516530910/d168744dex991.htm.

MINIMUM VIABLE PARAMETERS
Choose one tier or one rep/region and run a pilot.

SCALED PARAMETERS
Make sure everyone knows about your library of plays and how to use them.

MISTAKES TO AVOID
Don't be general. You can't be too specific in the breakdown of duties. Be clearer than clear.

Don't give up if your first play isn't a slam dunk.

Don't build a play without knowing what problem it's going to solve.

9

Activate

Remember Snowflake CEO Frank Slootman's mantra, "Execution beats strategy every day of the week"? Well, that idea is coming home to roost in this chapter. We've encouraged you to have a bias toward action all along, but this is the point in your one-team GTM learning curve where action is imperative.

It might feel daunting, but if you don't put these tactics into action now, you risk turning them into shelfware. We know because we've seen it happen.

Both of us have been consultants and advisers in our professional lives, which means we've been in the room with founders and heads of revenue who are trying to figure out how to put this type of go-to-market motion in place. And we've found that strategy is abundant and execution is woefully lacking. We've even encountered business leaders who—after spending months learning about ABM, creating internal systems, and planning plays—end up dwelling on all the reasons they can't take the plunge. They can give us a dozen reasons they can't launch these meticulously planned motions, and all we need from them is one reason they *can*.

If you're feeling hesitant, remember the idea of the two-way door: Trying out one-team GTM is low-risk, because if it doesn't suit your business, you can simply stop doing it. But you'll never know how well it could suit your business unless you try.

So let's get started.

Start with Cross-Functional Knowledge Sharing

As you begin to execute outreach in earnest, remember to stay in close communication with all stakeholders across your sales and marketing teams. If everyone retreats to their silos now, all your hard work will have been wasted. Creating a cohesive outbound motion requires you to collaborate around the orchestration of plays, bringing everyone together to coordinate details and align on execution.

Now more than ever, you need to think of yourselves as one big team.

And with that in mind, your first order of business in the activation process is to gather the players and make a plan together. Before you build any landing pages or schedule any sequences, gather all of the stakeholders on the accounts you plan to target. If at all possible, meet in person. This will be a true multi-way conversation where all people are involved, so don't send an email or ask them to fill out a form. Bring everyone together to facilitate genuine collaboration.

Quick side note: This process of meeting and coordinating can be applied to a deep dive into a single account for a one-to-one play, or it can cover a span of accounts for a one-to-many play. The rubric and the outcomes are the same; the meetings would just address different volumes of accounts.

Everyone needs to understand how the account or set of accounts has been engaged so far to ensure outreach is relevant and nonrepetitive. Multiple people will have insights to share, each from a different perspective. Look to the account owners first to understand if they have already engaged the account(s) in any way. If so, you want to determine what messages and topics have been used in communications thus far and if they have been successful, as well as if there are any political issues that need to be handled delicately.

Then, turn to marketing to lead a conversation regarding data insights that they prepared. These should include first- and third-party intent signals, product usage data if available, and any audience-specific learnings to keep in mind. Data can lead to many possible outcomes, so this should be a dynamic conversation to agree on which points are most relevant to guiding your campaign tactics. Next, look to the SDR to suggest messaging. What have they seen work in similar segments? With your messaging matrix in place from chapter 5, this should be straightforward.

At the end of this conversation you should have a clear understanding of:

The problem you believe you can solve in the segment/account's business. This is called the hypothesis of need.

Which product or solution you offer that will solve said problem

Who, in the account(s) you will collectively focus on (persona[s], line of business, subsidiary)

What message(s) you will use across the buying team you identified

Which content, if any, is recommended or requested from the sales team

Challenges and objections you expect to encounter along the way, internally and externally

Which tactics you want to employ, and who will be responsible for which, at what times

Scale Up: Once you have the motion in place, invite your field marketing and partner marketing teams to the table for this knowledge share. This is especially important in your 1-1 must-win accounts. Include them in your SLAs, measurement, and execution plan where it makes sense.

Make a plan to keep in touch with everyone as account outreach progresses—and don't forget to document everything being done—then prepare to activate. You've got your content ecosystem in place, a variety of possible plays you can use, and a sense of timing. Now, with your tailored hypothesis of need in hand, you're ready to launch.

Activate Your Content Experience

The ABM team typically begins activating the content experience by building a microsite or landing page for visitors from the target account. This will become the destination that everything else points to, from digital ads to SDR and sales emails, which is why it gets built out first. At Snowflake, it's a page with varying degrees of personalization, from the entire industry at minimum to the prospect's name and title on highly customized pages. We include a section encouraging visitors to connect with any questions, and a section with hand-picked content including invitations to webinars and live events, relevant in-house articles, demos, and case studies.

The knowledge-sharing session you had in the previous step will make or break the success of this content hub. It should determine which content, CTAs, and personalization elements get put on the page(s). We want everything in that final section to be as relevant and timely as possible so it will grab the attention of the visitor and provide tangible value to them.

The content will be most successful based on *your* data, but here is a content mix we recommend as a starting point. From here, look at your engagement and conversion metrics on your pages and run optimization experiments to further adjust.

Seven to twelve content pieces. Include a variety of formats like video, interactive, and PDF and a variety of content like competitive, partner-related, and relevant customer use cases. These assets are ungated because you already de-anonymized the visitor, which means you can track what they engage with.

Two or three CTAs. Include a variety of formats like in-person events, recorded webinars, and demand-centric options like joining the community or booking a demo.

Link to the sales rep's calendar to book time directly.

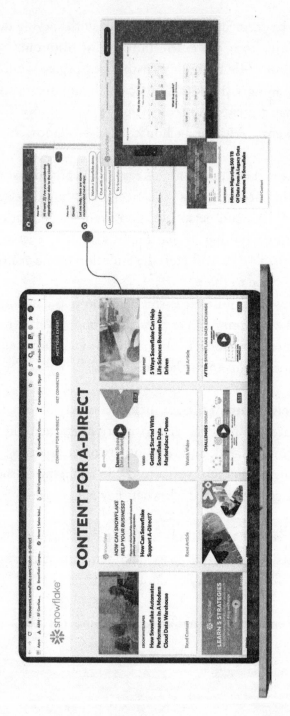

Content experience goes beyond curated assets. Think about interactions with chat, CTAs appropriate for the buying stage, and the opportunity to connect with an expert.

At the absolute minimum, the microsite must include at least one customer reference: a current customer of your company who has had success with your offerings. The idea here is to say to the visitor, "This other company loves working with us, and their needs are similar to yours. That's why we believe we'd be a great fit for you."

At scale, we include multiple tabs within the microsite, each of which leads to additional experiences by subsidiary or business unit so we can maintain relevance for each buying group.

Basic tech needed to activate content: Content Management System

Scaled tech needed to activate content: Content experience platform, meeting booking tool

Activate Your Digital Touch Points

At this point the ABM team will also prep a variety of digital touch points to ensure that the message you agreed upon is well-distributed across media the audience is visiting.

To make this possible, ABMers first agree on the value message and advertising copy with sales and ensure SDRs are aligned and in agreement as well. After all, the message needs to be consistent across sales, SDRs, and ABM for the impact to be recognized. ABMers also draw upon the knowledge-sharing conversation to determine which people within the account should receive which messages. More often than not, the AEs have a clear idea of what message they suggest starting with. This informs the audience-targeting variables in the digital campaign setup that need to be completed, such as functions, roles, titles, and skills. The ability to hyper-target different roles and functions is a major benefit to this approach. As one team, you may decide that sales wants to reserve C-suite targeting until an influencer is engaged, or target the C-suite with a business-level message while you target the influencer with a technical-level message. For example, if you serve one message to the entire segment or account, you will want any outreach to be appropriate to people working at other levels.

Channels for digital touch points may include:

Display advertising

In-mail messaging

Web personalization

Custom chat flows

Tailored webinars

| Email | Digital | Custom | Interactive | Virtual and |
| Banners | Advertising | Webpage | Chat | Physical mailers |

Consider a wide range of touchpoints across digital and physical channels that all echo a consistent message.

Again, these touch points will all point back to the microsite, whether to the landing page or individual asset hosted on it: ads, chat conversations, everything brings the visitor to the same spot. By funneling all of the traffic into that one page, you can make sure everyone from your target accounts is getting the right message at all times.

Basic tech needed to activate digital touch points: Digital advertising tool with account-targeting capabilities

Scaled tech needed to activate digital touch points: Chat tool that can be customized per account visiting the web page, web personalization and optimization tool, email signature banner tool, app-specific advertising accounts (Reddit, LinkedIn, etc.), virtual event hosting tool

---

INSIDE THE IGLOO WITH SNOWFLAKE:

Breanna Gaul, manager of account-based marketing for enterprise at Snowflake, on activation as a collaborative effort

The first hire to the ABM team at Snowflake five years ago, Breanna has seen this team grow from two people to our current global team of almost thirty. She has managed a team of six professional account-based marketers who are not only pushing the business to grow, but also leading the charge on what is possible in ABM. She has also led the creation of the Global ABM center of activation at Snowflake. In her work, she coordinates with sales to identify their most important accounts and to use multifaceted spearfishing techniques to target the right individuals at the right time and move their relationship with Snowflake forward.

We asked her to speak about the hardest part of ABM—execution—and how she has overcome challenges to get sales, SDRs, and ABM operating in unison.

We often see teams hesitate to implement a one-team GTM approach at the time of activation. When this happens, it's usually because one or more teams don't trust the data or fear that misaligned messaging will be used. Another common theme is teams feeling excited about the topic selected for messaging, but questioning their ability to speak to it in depth at the time of launch.

This is where the importance of establishing trust comes in. None of the teams should fear relinquishing control when working in a one-team approach, which is why we focus so much on relationship building. In my mind, ABM is 50 percent gaining cross-functional buy-in to rally support for proven programs, and 50 percent actually doing it. Activation is critical, of course, but it will never happen if you don't build that trust first. You have to learn to speak the language of your partners.

I believe the true key in learning to speak the language of your partners in sales is starting that relationship from a place of listening and learning. It is important to take the time to show your partners in sales that you care about their bottom line and the process they have to take to get there. Learn the ins and outs of the sales cycle at your company, learn to literally speak their language (terms like SQO, ACV, and quota) and finally, learn as much as you can about what truly drives them, a.k.a. what makes them money.

Really taking the time to learn these key points not only helps you to understand your partner and helps you to find common goals but also allows you to become the bridge between marketing and sales to drive the insane alignment needed for a truly successful one-team strategy.

That alignment is critically important since activation is all dependent on sales, SDR, and SDR Ops buy-in. When I was first starting, one of the sales managers who oversaw the Northeast region was really bought into the idea of ABM. His enthusiasm meant we could get the salespeople who reported to him to experiment with our team. At that time, the other regions were hesitant so we didn't partner with them as often, but once they saw what we were doing for the Northeast region they started to warm up to the idea. Having a champion in sales—that regional manager—who was articulating what we were doing in the value we had was game-changing. We wouldn't have been as successful if we didn't have him advocating for us on the other side.

Essentially, activation is about finding common ground to get off the ground.

Activate Your Offline Tactics

In addition to digital touch points and outreach, one-team GTM encompasses offline tactics like direct mail, events, and billboards. You want to make certain that complementary messages are showing up across all touch points, and ensuring everything connects back to your microsite or relevant CTA.

> **Events:** If sales and marketing are planning an event, all stakeholders will want to collaborate on the agenda, guest list, promotional materials, and venue design. Each stakeholder should coordinate their responsibilities to bring the event to fruition. At Snowflake, field marketing handles the event logistics like agenda, speakers, venue, and catering. ABM helps provide amplification via the digital touch points from the "Activate Your Digital Touch Points" section, and provides intent data to inform the event creation. AEs send invitations to their contacts and SDRs follow up before and after the event to schedule follow-on conversations with attendees. These physical events can be tailored to a single target account or address multiple accounts; may be run by your organization, a third party, or a partner; and can be physical or virtual.

Direct Mail: At Snowflake, we like to use direct mail as an extension of an event, as well as a touch point within a broader campaign. Regardless of how this piece of mail sits in the larger context, you must ensure that the swag or gift you're sending is relevant to the message you are trying to convey. When all is unboxed, the recipient should be reminded of your message, and the item itself should provide a sticking power unlike other media. You can consider adding a shortened URL or QR code printed with accompanying messaging, so recipients are once again pointed back to the microsite content experience created for them.

Out of Home: The sky's the limit on this one. No really: You could attach a banner behind an airplane and have it fly near your target account's headquarters if you wanted to. More realistically, you'll deploy media like digital and static billboards, or create an experience like hiring a food truck to serve lunch at your customer's campus. Out-of-home touch points offer a great opportunity to be creative and create experiences your customers will remember.

Regardless, you'll need to coordinate details of these activities with other teams, depending on the context of the activation. For direct mail, for example, the ABM and field marketing teams often work together to ideate the concept, ABM executes the logistics, sales teams nominate recipients, and SDRs conduct the outreach and follow-up.

Basic tech needed to activate offline tactics: Sequencing tool for follow-up, email tool for invitations, digital advertising tool for promotions

Scaled tech needed to activate offline tactics: Anything and everything you can think of!

Activate Your SDR Sequences

With the content and touch points ready to rock, it's time to prep the SDR team for action. This typically starts with a round of account research. Remember that SDRs are uniquely suited to researching companies and applying what they find to highly personal and relevant messages that build on the hypothesis of need for the play.

Once everyone has agreed to the hypothesis of need in the knowledge-sharing meeting, and while the ABM team is building various types of content, SDRs begin conducting research on the accounts targeted by the upcoming plays. They've already got templated sequences prepped, but sequences are just starting points. They serve as foundational building blocks that remove the repetitive work SDRs will do for every account and free up time to focus on tailoring messages. SDRs are looking for any references to the account they can drop into the templated sequence to customize it, ideally tidbits that allow for personalization at *at least* the company level for one-to-many plays, and at the individual level for more focused plays at higher-value accounts.

As they research, key things that SDRs should be looking for include:

Executive Quotes: Relevant things the CEO said recently, snippets from leadership that have appeared in online articles, etc. Show them you know them by referencing what they've said.

Company Facts: This can include everything from news coverage about the company or its market to facts and figures about the company's health.

Comparison Cases: Identifying similar customers can help an SDR strengthen their outreach. Again, the idea here is to say, "This other company loves working with us, and their needs are similar to yours . . ." Companies want to know what their competition is up to.

Current Competitive Environment: Understand the current competitive environment within the account. What vendors are in place? When are their renewals up? Are there complementary solutions that can amplify your solution's value?

SDRs typically do this research in collaboration with their sales counterpart, ensuring that all findings reinforce the hypothesis of need. Account research can be done at any funnel stage, but if teams are working on a prospecting play then everything we've described above is particularly relevant.

There are a variety of ways that SDRs can catalog the research they find. At the most basic level, they can maintain a spreadsheet with facts and findings about each account. At an advanced level, you can build fields directly into the sales engagement platform to track these details and automatically pull them into sequence emails and social messages.

With research complete (or in progress), email writing begins. Email writing is an art, but there is a science behind it when you use a strategic touch point framework and custom variables to remind yourself to personalize. The email below sits at the start of Snowflake's Data Engineering sequence, and shows some examples of how we position Snowflake messaging among other important variables.

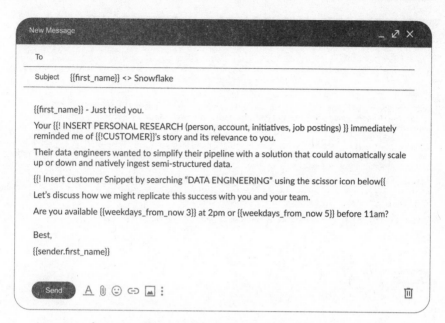

New Message   _ ⬈ ✕

To

Subject   {{first_name}} <> Snowflake

{{first_name}} - Just tried you.

Your {{! INSERT PERSONAL RESEARCH (person, account, initiatives, job postings) }} immediately reminded me of {{!CUSTOMER}}'s story and its relevance to you.

Their data engineers wanted to simplify their pipeline with a solution that could automatically scale up or down and natively ingest semi-structured data.

{{! Insert customer Snippet by searching "DATA ENGINEERING" using the scissor icon below{{

Let's discuss how we might replicate this success with you and your team.

Are you available {{weekdays_from_now 3}} at 2pm or {{weekdays_from_now 5}} before 11am?

Best,

{{sender.first_name}}

Send   A 📎 ☺ 🔗 🖼 ⋮   🗑

Automate the repeatable parts of emails while providing "in the moment" directions for your SDRs to personalize.

Another way to approach emails within a sequence is to break each into its component parts. The subject line is incredibly important, because as anyone knows, emails that never get opened never get read. Next comes the hook, which is an unignorable positioning statement or attention-grabbing fact that the reader sees the instant they open the email. It should contain some strategic personalization: Ask yourself, "Would the reader immediately feel that a human wrote this specifically for them?" The value proposition describes how your product has helped companies similar to the reader's company and explains exactly how your product made a difference. The final note is a call to action prompting the reader to take a clear and specific action.

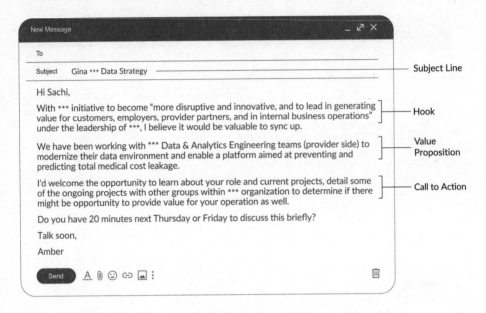

An example of a highly account-based email directly referencing
executive priorities and firsthand knowledge of the company's priorities.
Redacted for privacy.

It's worth noting that this formula for creating email templates ties back to best practices we've already discussed.

The value proposition section is meant to describe for the reader a scenario that they want to see unfold; something that might get them promoted. This section says to them, "If you buy our product and it creates this outcome, you'll look good, your job will be easier, and your business will succeed." It should contain a message of this kind that will resonate with anyone who falls into one of the persona groups you built in chapter 5.

The subject line, hook, and call to action can all function as check engine lights for the SDR team. If the email isn't being opened, you probably need to revisit your subject line. If opens are failing to generate replies, that call to action isn't working.

The beautiful thing is that sales engagement platforms typically have A/B testing for every component of the email built right into the tool. At Snowflake, we have at least one alternative version of each email component running at any given time for optimization purposes. Remember statistics 101 and only test changes to a single variable at a time. If you want to find a more effective subject line, then deploy an exact clone of an existing email and only alter the subject line. The version with the better open rate wins and makes room for another experiment. By the way, this optimization becomes impossible if you fail to control who creates sequences within your organization, as we mentioned in chapter 6.

Basic tech needed to activate SDR sequences: sales engagement platform

Scaled tech needed to activate SDR sequences: live chat solution, video recording tool, direct mail provider, contact data providers

Activate Your Measurement

Now that you're activating, let's bring to bear the account funnel with inspection metrics we introduced in chapter 3.

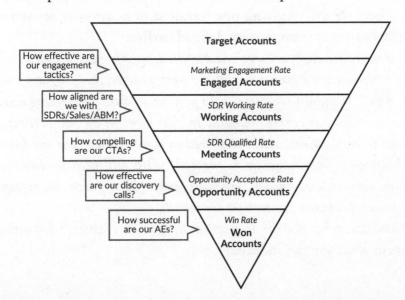

Well, it's relevant again now that you're activating. We cannot emphasize this strongly enough: You must know which metric you're tracking before you launch anything. Otherwise you'll have no idea if you succeeded or failed or how to improve on your performance the next time around.

Don't let anything go live or get sent without first agreeing on measures of success. What will you track? Where will you see it? How will you pull reports summarizing your results? What tech do you need to do this? Do you have the right mechanisms in place? Have you set a goal?

Do not pass "go" before answering these questions. A more formulaic way to determine what success looks like collectively (and by team) is to frame metrics like a hypothesis:

If we achieve [metric] *by* [date], *this program was successful. This result represents X increase over the baseline of* [metric].

To achieve this, the ABM team needs to achieve [metric] *by* [date], *the SDR team needs to complete* [metric] *by* [date], *and sales needs to complete* [metric] *by* [date].

Each person/team's responsibilities can be found here [link to project plan with agreed-upon SLAs].

Here is what this looks like, completed, for an example project where we are targeting one hundred noncustomer accounts in the healthcare segment we defined earlier:

If we collectively achieve one hundred completed SDR meetings in the Healthcare segment during the next quarter, this program was successful. The result represents a 43 percent account-to-meeting rate, which exceeds our current baseline in that segment by 400 percent.

In order to do this, ABM will need to move eighty of the one hundred accounts from unaware to engaged, SDRs will need to sequence twenty contacts/account/day, and sales will need to reach out to two VP/C-Level contacts per account per month.

You can reference the inspection metrics in chapter 3 for some ideas of what you can measure.

Basic tech needed to activate measurement: CRM system with native reporting

Scaled tech needed to activate measurement: data cloud platform and an analytics/visualization solution or an ABM platform

Activate Your Plays

The moment of truth is here: It's time to combine content, timing, and strategy to roll out your plays. Stakeholders from both sales and marketing are poised and ready to catalyze all of your collaborative prep work and begin reaching out to target accounts.

Here's how this comes together at Snowflake for our Snowmobile one-to-many program:

| | | New Quarter | | |
Quarterly Meeting with Sales/ABM/SDR Manager to select themes	Quarter 0 (Previous Quarter)	Quarter 1	Quarter 2	Quarter 3
Solution/Vertical 1	ABM Account Selection | Ads | Contact Enrichment	SDR Outbound 20+ contacts per week		
Solution/Vertical 2		ABM Account Selection | Ads | Contact Enrichment	SDR Outbound 20+ contacts per week	
Solution/Vertical 3			ABM Account Selection | Ads | Contact Enrichment	SDR Outbound 20+ contacts per week
Solution/Vertical 1 (Next Quarter)				ABM Account Selection | Ads | Contact Enrichment

*Marketing should always be preparing campaigns ahead of sales
outreach in order to turn cold calling to "warm calling."*

It all starts with a quarterly meeting among sales, ABM, and SDR leadership to prioritize segments, determine outreach themes for the quarter, and agree on hypotheses of need. The meeting takes place at least six weeks before the new quarter begins, and the themes are influenced by intent data, account commonalities, sales knowledge, and business priorities. For example, if four customers in our healthcare segment have been searching for terms like "database" and "patient data privacy," we might craft a quarterly outreach campaign around those themes. Segments and themes are prioritized and separated into workloads/verticals, then everyone gets to work on building strategic content and outreach plans around those themes.

One month before the new quarter begins, the ABM team creates and begins auditing the database to ensure the proper nature and volume of contacts is available for sales and SDRs, enlisting third-party sources as needed. They then nail down the messaging and content that will be used across teams and touch points. They build microsites and launch digital tactics like display advertising, all of which connect to the first theme. As soon as the new quarter begins, the SDR team begins outreach to the accounts that have now seen and engaged with the promoted content, preparing them for eventual contact from sales.

Meanwhile, ABM has moved on to the *second* solution/vertical and is getting those accounts ready for SDR contact, and so on. As the quarter comes to an end, the leaders meet again, pick new segments and themes, and the process starts from the top.

The work that we're doing in month 1 of any given quarter may not lead to a closed sale for many months to come. But if we didn't do it that far in advance, we'd make it much harder for a salesperson to close that sale. The entire waterfall is designed to continually fill the sales pipeline.

Basic tech needed to activate plays: Minimum from all of the above

Scaled tech needed to activate plays: Scaled from all of the above

At this point, you've tackled the basics of executing one-team GTM at startup speed, and you're beginning the exciting process of revving up toward enterprise scale. In the coming chapters, we'll explore how to continue expanding your program in sustainable and effective ways.

MINIMUM VIABLE ACTIVATION
At least the SDR activation, plus at least one of the other three activations detailed in this chapter.

SCALED ACTIVATION
All of what we've outlined in this chapter, on continuous repeat.

MISTAKES TO AVOID
Don't start without knowing how you'll measure success.

Don't give the same level of activation to every play type. Higher-priority accounts can get more effort.

Don't skip meeting with sales and understanding exactly where they're at with the account.

PART 4
SCALE

10

Build Your Organization

Both of us were hired by Snowflake to expand functions and build out our teams, tech, and strategies. We were tasked with building organizations within the larger organization.

We're not telling you this because we think our own career stories are riveting. Instead, we want to make the point that scaling an organization doesn't just happen because you've been hired to do it. It happens because you logically and passionately build a case for doing it in close coordination with influencers and decision-makers in the business.

Hillary was brought on to scale Snowflake's ABM program, but also to connect the ABM team to the SDRs more directly. She was meant to be a bridge-builder. When she arrived, she quickly learned that, while leadership's directive for change was helpful and was already in place, she needed to win the hearts and minds of her direct team and cross-functional peers. Change is not easy, and Hillary knew the process required having a vision, a why, and a digestible plan for how to achieve her vision. If the company's goal was one big team, why should the teams care and how will they know it was worth it? Let's face it, it's often easier to work in silos in the near term, but it's extremely inefficient and unproductive for long-term impact. She knew it was worth the investment to build bridges early on, ensuring the solutions she was putting into place solved real problems for others in the business.

After scouring all the ABM resources and templates she could find, Hillary slowly moved from textbook frameworks to robust, integrated plays unique to Snowflake. She started by standardizing the team's SLAs, creating clear sets of deliverables and desired outcomes, with insight and enablement around what sales needed to contribute and KPIs that would determine success. This was key to establishing trust, the foundation of a strong cross-functional relationship. With consistent measurement, she could then start evaluating what was working compared to the business goals, and what could be optimized.

Next, she dove into the SDR relationship, working to understand the current landscape, appetite for collaboration, and opportunities to overlap their efforts for multiplied impact. Through trial and error, she learned that the best path forward was to start small, try one idea and one collaboration play in a single sales region, and *then* scale it to the broader SDR and ABM teams. This allowed her to collect data to demonstrate impact, then build on it with additional data as the program grew and additional resources were needed.

Travis was hired to start an entirely new function at Snowflake: dedicated operations and enablement for the sales development team. His first major project was creating a big-picture view of the setup of the existing SDR organization. At the time, the business was wrapping up the process of increasing efficiencies and resource allocation in anticipation of its blockbuster IPO. That exercise resulted in a sales development team that was stretched thin, with each SDR supporting an average of seven to eight account executives. This setup posed an intuitive challenge for an organization of junior salespeople. They had to navigate the personalities, business preferences, and communication styles of many tenured sales professionals with decades of experience. There wasn't enough time to dedicate even one working day per week to each supported AE. But intuition doesn't justify major strategic decisions like growing head count.

Travis had to prove that intentionally staffing up SDRs would help Snowflake realize its vision of an integrated marketing motion that was account-based, data driven, sophisticated, and scalable. He also had to prove the return on investment that each incremental SDR would yield to his own bosses and, eventually, the C-suite. The proposal took a great deal of analytical work and careful iteration of the presentation narrative, but it ultimately led to funding an acceleration of the SDR function and improving rep productivity for the ensuing quarters.

Our own relationship was forged while we were building our teams, tech, and strategies. Hillary had the domain expertise in ABM to know what it should look like at scale, and Travis had the operational expertise to build repeatable prospecting systems and processes. We went from casually introducing ourselves on a Zoom call to unloading our respective hopes and dreams for what a true one-team GTM approach looked like. As we vented with phrases like "that standard practice never made sense to me" and "if only," we quickly realized that we each held the solution to the other's problems. Great account-based marketing requires great sales development, and vice versa.

In this chapter, we'll walk you through doing that yourself. For the purpose of this book, we will focus on scaling the ABM and SDR teams in response to the sales team growth and needs. We'll help you make the case for scaling your efforts and show you how to get the head count, budget, and buy-in you need to expand your unified dream team.

Adding Head Count to Your Team

Before you start writing job descriptions or allocating budget dollars to new hires, consider how you want your ABM and SDR teams to be organized. How will you structure your teams? How many managers or leaders do you need, and where will they sit in the org chart? This is especially important in scaling ABM/SDR programs since you are still in silo-busting mode: the hires you plan to make can be overseen by several different leaders across the sales and marketing org. Where you place them may affect the amount of friction or support they (and you) experience. We are intentionally sidestepping the topic of sales head count planning as that could be an entire book itself, and we don't have the space to properly cover it here.

For example, many companies choose to have their SDR teams report to sales. They are performing sales development work, so it seems natural to keep them with other sales functions. However, at Snowflake our SDRs and ABMers are both consolidated under marketing, and marketing has been assigned the charter of pipeline generation. This unlocked our ability to execute the integrated prospecting motions we've outlined in this book, the one-two punch of surgically targeted marketing efforts followed by intentional human touch points. Ultimately SDRs will thrive under the organization most passionate and understanding of the function.

Another alignment consideration is the division of labor within sales. Are your AEs responsible for a specific region or a vertical? To scale marketing's alignment with sales, consider segmenting marketing resources by whatever model sales uses. At Snowflake, we organize ABM, the SDRs, and field marketing by the same rubric as sales. In our case, this is primarily by industry verticals and regional territories.

And harkening back to chapter 4, we recommend building and scaling your teams according to the segmentation you've already done. Generally speaking, higher-value account tiers justify higher investment and attention from the organization. On the SDR side, you should consider a denser coverage ratio for your sales team that targets your most strategic accounts relative to the sales team that focuses on mid-market accounts. If you have a "hunter/ farmer" account segmentation—one sales team acquires new logos while another retains and expands customers—consider staffing up SDRs for the new logo team at a faster pace than your expansion team.

As your team of SDRs grows, we encourage you to add an SDR operations position to your org chart. Most companies have sales ops and sales enablement teams who support the AEs. These individuals or teams define the processes, handle AE reporting needs, and generally remove friction from the selling process. When these same companies hire a sales development team, they do so understanding that prospecting can be separate from selling . . . but they often task an SDR manager with the long list of operational duties that remove friction from the lives of the SDR team.

Why is this a bad idea for scale? Your average SDR is early in their career and therefore requires a higher level of enablement and coaching. They are among the most tool-heavy members of your entire GTM team, often juggling as many as eighteen pieces of software per day. That tech stack spits out an incredible volume of data that requires close analysis and summary. Even with these factors, organizations put all operational and enablement duties on the shoulders of the SDR manager in addition to their core job of hiring great talent, leading their team, and coordinating with their sales counterparts.

Once you have two SDR managers and about twenty people in the SDR org, that's when you can justify an ops and/or enablement position. Adding this expert to your SDR team frees up SDR leaders to hire, coach, execute, and promote their people. (And be good collaborators on all the plays we've talked about.) If SDR ops didn't exist, Snowflake couldn't have scaled as quickly and successfully as it did.

INSIDE THE IGLOO WITH SNOWFLAKE:

Lars Nilsson, VP of global sales development at Snowflake, on SDR ops as a must-have

With more than twenty-five years of sales and operations experience in the technology sector, Lars Nilsson is a global leader in enterprise software and selling solutions. Prior to Snowflake, Lars was CEO of Sales Source, a premier revenue operations consulting firm specializing in industry-leading best practices and advisory for the optimization and build-out of sales operations and inside sales teams. Prior to that, he was the VP of global inside sales for Cloudera. Lars and his team at Cloudera developed the sales methodology account-based sales development (ABSD), which has transformed how businesses approach high-value targets. As special adviser at True Ventures, Lars helps True portfolio companies implement best-of-breed sales technologies and processes enabling efficient revenue operations. His unique blend of leadership skills and sales acumen has benefited dozens of startups in the Valley and beyond. Mentoring sales teams is one of his greatest passions.

We asked him to speak about how SDR operations can make or break an ABM/SDR collaboration.

What a lot of people don't realize about building an SDR team is that you can come up with a best practice, create a blueprint, or write a playbook and throw it over to a handful of willing and able, fire-in-the-belly SDRs. They will run with it and find success. But what happens over time, is you realize it is working and now you've got to scale your practice. When you get to ten, and then twenty, and then one hundred SDRs on your team, you need more operational rigor and oversight. SDRs, if given the opportunity, will be eager to try something new and consequently will "go off script."

You need an SDR-dedicated ops function, because a single SDR manages more procedure, more policy, and more technology than almost anyone else. If you count up the number of apps and technologies that SDRs use, it's somewhere between thirteen and eighteen different systems that they're in every day: two or three times more than a seller. Because of this, they need more operations, enablement, and training. They need the consistent support that ops provides in order to thrive, and when they thrive the business thrives.

Devoid of this role, the enablement, the onboarding, and the training falls to the frontline SDR manager or a learning and development team too far removed from the SDR daily responsibilities.

While critical for scale, not all SDR teams need an ops or enablement person. You have to have maturity in marketing and sales, and an SDR team that has been through some level of scale, success, and awareness. You need to be committed to doing it with operational rigor and create an environment where you leave nothing to chance. If you do this right, and support your team with ops and enablement when you scale, you can accelerate pipeline and revenue growth with SDRs.

And that growth is amplified by ABM. I led an SDR team without marketing at a previous company, but it didn't work as well or as fast as it does here at Snowflake. The partnership of ABM reps together with SDRs turned out to be the magic ingredient, and what has blown this thing wide open. I've been evangelizing for SDRs, but now I want to start evangelizing for whatever it's called when you have ABM and SDRs working together.

On the ABM side, alignment should follow the same sales-assignment pattern as the SDR organization, but with a higher ratio of ABMers to AEs than SDRs to AEs. While ABM can cover a higher number of sales reps for one-to-many programs, highly strategic one-to-one requires a lower ratio, so you will want to map your coverage accordingly based on your initiatives. The biggest time constraint for ABM is the time needed to meet with the selling team to truly understand their accounts, take part in sales leadership meetings, and play a role in account strategy across GTM teams. Because of that, we recommend using technology to scale wherever possible, leaving the human resources for use on the things that humans do best: relationship-building and cross-functional strategy.

When you start out, a single ABM hire can establish a preliminary program with the sales team. There are two paths you can take. One is to start with a more senior-level person who will take the top ten accounts across the entire sales org as well as some one-to-many programs. This person can establish a baseline, then hire out a team as the value of ABM is proven and resources are made available.

This strategy works well if you have definitive buy-in from your leadership team to invest in seasoned talent and are open to your new ABM lead both building and defining the rest of the organization from there.

Alternatively, if you have fewer financial resources or are still building momentum on the whole ABM thing, you can hire an eager, more junior candidate to cover a single segment. This segment is most likely to be your must-win or Fortune 200 accounts that are more robust in nature, with multiple subsidiaries and complex buying cycles. Once that individual has made some headway, you can start adding additional head count by segment or territory.

By the time you've hired three ABMers, we recommend looking for a player-coach that can manage the team moving forward while also being responsible for their own territory. When you get to five head count, you will benefit from an ABM lead who does *not* own a territory and is fully responsible for program development, measurement, and management of the team. Whether you start with a senior ABM hire or build from a more junior baseline, you will eventually need to have them report into your growth marketing organization. It is also common for the team to report into demand gen, which is only problematic if the leadership of that group doesn't buy into the idea of accounts versus leads for ABM measurement. If the newly formed ABM team is set up to be measured by leads, they are set up to fail.

Like any seamless business function, ops and enablement are equally important. When starting out, this can sometimes be handled by a seasoned ABM leader with strong operational skills who will be critical to building the org from the ground up. If you're not going to serve as ABM ops yourself, figure out who will be doing it. Is there a marketing ops function that can help support the ABM team? Who will oversee processes and admin duties as you scale?

If your ABM program grows enough to go global, consider pushing beyond a few ops people to creating an operational center of excellence. This team would be responsible for creating consistent and structured lessons and enablement; documented plays that can be replicated; use cases that are valuable across multiple teams; and other codified guides.

One final note on head count: Pay attention to ratios of support. As we mentioned at the beginning of this chapter, asking one SDR to support eight AEs is a recipe for disaster. So is expecting a newly minted three-person ABM team to fulfill the needs of a few hundred seasoned salespeople. As you scale your go-to-market functions, make sure you don't overpromise what your growing teams can accomplish.

With your plan to add head count in hand, your next move is to secure the funds to start hiring. Let's talk budget asks.

Securing Budget for Your ABM and SDR Programs

Requesting money is never easy or simple, even if you're in charge of expanding your programs. Our advice may not be groundbreaking, but it will definitely help you approach this tough task strategically.

To start, create a detailed list of what you need to scale up and augment the program you've already built. For new staff salaries, look at market-based pay reports to rough out some figures. Managerial positions may not have as much benchmarking in these reports, but salaries for ABM or SDR managers should be similar to marketing or sales manager salaries respectively. Research and account for commissions if they apply as well as soft costs like benefits and PTO; many experts use the rule of thumb that total employee cost is typically 1.25 to 1.4 times the salary.[1]

---

1   Weltman, Barbara. "How Much Does an Employee Cost You?" U.S. Small Business Administration. August 22, 2019. https://www.sba.gov/blog/how-much-does-employee-cost-you.

Since you'll be making the case for these new hires, lead the budget request with ROI calculations. How much pipeline lift will adding three new SDRs create? What lift do you expect ABM to create for sales, SDRs, and cross-functional marketing?

Next consider the plays themselves. You need subscriptions to data provision services, money to power digital advertising, budget to try new tactics unique to an account-based approach, and more. By this point, you've run a handful of plays, so you know approximately how much it costs per account to run those plays. Ballpark how many of each play you hope to run over the coming year, and multiply by the number of accounts who'll get that treatment.

Once you know the cost per account, remember that ABM is a long-tail approach with multifaceted contribution, so connecting ROI directly to spend is more challenging than traditional tactics. Hillary breaks it down by engagement and pipeline generation: "Engaged accounts are X percent more successful at Y KPI than non-engaged accounts."

If at all possible, allot around 5 percent of your ABM budget to innovation and experimentation. Especially for a function as fluid and fast-moving as ABM, it's helpful to set aside a pool of money dedicated to trying new things that may or may not be extremely impactful, so the team can continue evolving. It helps everyone explore the real gamut of options instead of playing it safe, which can lead to some unexpected wins, and it's fantastic for team morale. At Snowflake, some of our most successful programs have come from this approach.

Finally, add any costs for tech and tools you'll need to equip your team for success. If you are just starting out, account for the growth of tools you already have. If you are scaling, consider new technologies that will enable your team to operate across more accounts more efficiently and reduce manual inputs.

For every ask, there must be a justification. Do your best to add supporting data and value explanations for every request. It never hurts to get a handful of stats from third parties about the efficacy of ABM/SDR programs, but we suggest leaning heavily on evidence taken from your own efforts. Some leaders are most interested in seeing how the work has impacted your own company and find external facts and figures irrelevant. Show them what you've done and paint a picture of how you plan to build on your successes.

Here's how you can structure that argument and convince company leaders to support expansion.

Making Your Case

Hopefully you've secured buy-in from key stakeholders as you've laid all the groundwork for your first few plays and run them. Now, however, you've got to get buy-in from someone who can fund the expansion of this work. It can be nerve-racking, we know. Your best bet is to be as prepared as possible to make a strong case.

Start with the absolute basics.

What case are you trying to make?

You want to build on the ABM/SDR work you've done so far, and scale your nascent program. To do that, you need head count and budget.

To whom do you need to make your case?

Consider this carefully, as you may not need to book time with the CEO or CFO. Ask yourself, "Who's the one allocating budget at my level?" Or if you're facing a budgetary bottleneck, who is blocking you? The fact is you simply need buy-in from someone who holds budget on the GTM side, and has enough influence to help you build out the organization you're envisioning. In all likelihood, that someone is in your own area, whether that's sales or marketing. As you ponder this, also consider when various stakeholders set their budgets and plan to speak with them a few months earlier. You definitely don't want to make your ask after the annual budget's been set.

How can you make your case?

You've already got some org chart input sketched out and a rough idea of how much money you'll need to make changes, so much of the legwork is already done. If they're not already fully supportive, get the person directly above you bought in. Convince the next person up in the hierarchy—likely whomever you report to—that expanding the ABM/SDR organization will benefit everyone. Including them: No harm in emphasizing how fantastic *they* will look when this program starts raking in the revenue.

If your boss doesn't control the budget you need, encourage them to take the message and carry it up the chain of command. Ask how you can support them in doing so. Make sure the case for expansion will travel through leadership ranks until it reaches whoever controls the budget you need to access.

In a best-case scenario, your boss will call on you to present the idea yourself. If this happens, you'll need to do some prep work: research the leader to whom you'll be presenting. What do they care about most in the business? What is their vision for growth and expansion? Build a presentation that proves you know how to put that vision into place, and build your case around that. As you research, also investigate how complete your plan should be before you offer it up. We know that certain executives prefer to have information given to them slowly over time and their input incorporated. Others require a fully formed and thoroughly vetted plan up front, or they'll reject it out of hand. Know your audience before you prep your argument.

Be sure to incorporate your metrics and data, regardless of the format in which you choose to share it. As we said earlier, a couple of third-party stats might help, but you should lean more heavily on your own data. To get enthusiastic buy-in, you need to prove that one-team GTM is working *in house* and *right now*. And also prove that it ties back to your *why*: If you're pursuing it to catalyze massive growth, tie your metrics to that. If you're pursuing account-based strategies to enter new markets, show how your initial experiments created penetration. Whatever it is, link the ideas to the numbers.

Finally, feel free to use the arguments we make in this book to persuade others! You're already convinced that a robust and growing one-team GTM program will benefit your business. Combine that enthusiasm with the cases, stats, and assertions we've made in these pages, and you can't go wrong.

Before we close out this chapter, we want to circle back to head count for a moment. You're standing at a crossroads right now, and about to bring some more people into the ABM/SDR fold to work with you. Especially since those people will be involved in growing this effort, try to hire people who have a vision. They need to know where they're taking this work, why, and how. Both of us look for people who are operationally minded, obsessed with innovation, naturally collaborative, and capable of independent thought. People like that not only create processes, they improve existing processes. They don't need to be micromanaged because they're driven and self-directed, constantly looking for ways to improve their work and move the organization forward.

Stack your team roster with operationally minded innovators, and everything you do will get better with each passing quarter. They'll make sure of it.

Stack your team roster with collaborators, and busting silos will be a breeze. Good thing, too, since our next order of business is to explore cross-functional marketing.

MINIMUM VIABLE ORGANIZATION
Defined goals for one-team GTM efforts

At least one person on each the marketing, sales and SDR teams who are bought in and charging toward a one-team GTM approach

Enablement owned by people leaders in marketing, sales and SDR teams

SCALED ORGANIZATION
Multiple dedicated ABM resources aligned to the same regions or segments as sales and SDRs, reporting to a dedicated ABM leader

Dedicated SDR Operations & Enablement function

Scale-ready tech stack to increase capacity of personalization

Predictable ROI for incremental head count growth

MISTAKES TO AVOID
Overinvesting in sales head count in advance of SDRs and marketing

Asking for head count budget before securing an internal one-team GTM champion

Segmenting SDRs and marketers differently than the sales organization

11

Learn to Love Cross-Functional Marketing

Adding new team members isn't the only way to scale what you've built so far. In fact, if you aren't confident that you can secure a budget for additional head count, or have the head count and are ready for what's next, you can take another approach to scaling: collaborating across marketing functions.

(Side note: We understand that some of you work at companies with some combination of demand gen, field marketing, product marketing, and partner marketing folded into a single role. This chapter is all about scaling across those functions, so feel free to skip ahead if your marketing org simply isn't specialized yet.)

Why consider a cross-functional strategy? Because it amplifies the investments you've already made. It allows you to get even more groups working in concert. Each of those groups may be delivering a variety of calls to action, which gives recipients a broader range of connection points to choose from: If they aren't interested in a webinar, they might still attend an in-person event. By giving them more choices, you create more chances to grab their attention. And on top of that, everyone benefits from increased focus, and focus comes from collaborating around a shared list of accounts. There's a natural lift that happens when partner teams support each other and pool their resources, and much of that has to do with everyone aiming for the same target.

But a quick word of warning: you'll have more luck forging internal partnerships if you can prove that your one-team GTM motion is already working.

Hillary knows this from personal experience. She tried to go cross-functional in her first ninety days at Snowflake before she'd really gotten enough successful plays under her belt to prove she was onto something big. The problem was, she hadn't taken the rest of the teams along the journey of discovery with her, to build trust and gain buy-in. You not only need collaboration to do that, you need data to drive vision, with thoughtfully planned tactics that include those teams in the ideation, execution, and measurement.

Building cross-functional breadth of programs is a great way to multiply the impact of your programs, but first, you need to establish depth of your account-based programs, with multiple KPIs and inspection metrics. Then you need to listen to the needs of the organization before prescribing tactics at large. In other words, you need to nail the first two parts of this book. At Snowflake, we now include cross-functional components in just about everything that we do, and also include relative metrics each quarter in our business reviews. Once you've established those relationships and extended your one-team GTM approach to the entire marketing org, you and your colleagues can start to create some creative, fun, and wildly successful cross-functional plays.

Let's start by exploring which teams you can collaborate with.

Cross-Functional Collaboration with Demand Generation

You may know the demand-gen team as your company's ongoing interest-boosting, account-nurturing, lead-generating machine. Because of that—and because they are constantly capturing and qualifying leads—they are the main source of first-party data and first-party engagements that we can use to kick off and initiate plays for ABM, SDRs and sales.

Since we've asked you *not* to measure your account-based work by leads generated, we want to clarify that leads are an inspection metric for this group. They're looking at self-service sign-ups, free trials, virtual hands-on lab sign-ups, and demos—things that, by their very nature, create leads. But demand gen doesn't determine their success by the volume of those leads alone. They evaluate the impact of those leads as part of the broader efforts concentrated on accounts they serve alongside other marketing functions.

Demand gen is responsible for: Generating campaign responses from the personas most relevant to the business offerings.

Primary inspection metric: Qualified responses

At Snowflake, our demand-gen team doesn't measure volume alone. In addition to inspection metrics like cost per assigned lead (CPAL) and SLAs generated and accepted, they measure an account-centric metric: **percentage of qualified leads from target accounts**. This means that if ten thousand people show up to an event, this team ultimately wants to know how many of those people match our target account universe. Not all engagement is meaningful, so they want to ensure they don't get misled by vanity metrics. They're measuring their results and setting their goals based on the engagement they are generating in the account universe that is owned by sales, in addition to broader persona engagement. Not all demand-gen teams use this measurement system, but we love it for our own work. It makes alignment with the ABM and SDR teams far easier and more natural and down-funnel results more predictable.

Another thing we love about this particular collaboration is that it quickly becomes cyclical. Demand gen starts focusing its efforts on stimulating responses in accounts; SDRs and ABM can then use demand gen as a call to action to stimulate *more* demand in the accounts; which stimulates more engagement; which stimulates more focus. It creates an incredible positive feedback loop.

How ABM Works with Demand Gen: The baseline for this collaboration is for ABM and the SDR team to home in on a small group within the larger group that demand gen is targeting. For example, imagine that Snowflake is planning a webinar for a specific use case. Demand gen will create messaging that will be broadcast to all possible accounts who might benefit from the webinar. But ABM and the SDR team can take that a step further and create highly customized content and messaging for a subset of accounts (also nominated by sales as tier 1 or tier 2 accounts). In this case, we already have ABM campaigns in-flight that we can incorporate demand-gen components into.

For the sake of this example, let's say the demand-gen team is hosting a webinar for data science leaders in financial services. You know that you have forty-seven accounts in financial services that you are targeting with ABM already, and they're relying on data science for the next evolution of their product development. This is a great opportunity to add a CTA to your forty-seven accounts' microsites that points them to a registration page for the demand gen–hosted webinar.

You can also incorporate outreach from SDRs in their existing touch sequence that encourages data scientists from these target accounts to register. You can then launch digital advertisements promoting this event to those forty-seven accounts either as a one-to-many tactic with the same messaging, or break them down into smaller cohorts for even more specific messaging as to how they can benefit from the content.

Simultaneously, you can connect with your sales reps to understand which contacts they have in those forty-seven accounts and encourage them to send a personal invitation from their own email and follow up based on attendance. If one of their contacts didn't attend? Have them send a "We missed you" note, and leverage a piece of targeted direct mail as an offer. If one of their contacts did attend? Have sales reach out to them with next steps and offer to continue the conversation.

Although the campaign and webinar originate with demand gen, the ABM team may put a different flavor on their messaging for this audience. The SDRs might use a specific angle for this industry. Both teams are taking the giant list of accounts that demand gen has selected, narrowing focus, and speaking even more directly to those folks.

On a related note, the goal of SDR collaboration in this type of activity with demand gen is *not* to replace a marketing automation system. Instead, it's to add a level of personal messaging and customization that's the hallmark of this motion. Their role is to harness the buzz that demand gen has created, tailor it, make it personal, and deliver it. They're best suited at personally engaging buyers in accounts, so be sure to focus their energies there.

Example Play

Straight-to-Meeting Initiative: Traditionally in marketing, demand generation will generate qualified leads that SDRs follow up on using calling and messaging touch points after the fact. However, with modern technology and a slick outbound GTM machine, you can get ahead of the curve and make the connection for a valuable conversation *before* a virtual or physical demand-gen event takes place. While this helps eliminate a flurry of post-event follow-up calls, it also allows the prospect or customer to take initiative when they are ready, instead of waiting for a phone call from a stranger.

Who You're Talking To (Personas): Focus your efforts on individuals who register for landmark events you are hosting. Think customer conferences, marquee prospect in-person events, or important virtual events like demos.

What you're telling them (message): Offer the opportunity to connect with an expert ahead of the event to gain additional context and have a personalized conversation.

How you will communicate the message (content): The content is limited to the language you use to encourage the registrant to book a meeting.

How you will deliver the message (SDR plays, marketing channels): Surface your SDR's or AE's calendar on the registration confirmation page so that registrants can book a time that works for them if they are interested. Or even speak to them at the physical event itself. If they choose not to book, initiate an AE or SDR touch sequence leading up to the event.

Timing: Trigger the calendar immediately upon event registration. Trigger the SDR or AE touch point within one hour of event registration.

Goals: The benefit of this approach is twofold. First, it reduces friction for prospects and customers to enter a conversation easily and quickly. Second, it reduces time-to-meeting by starting touch points before the event instead of after.

Cross-Functional Collaboration with Field Marketing

At Snowflake, we call this team the "eyes and ears of the field." They handle everything from live events to physical activation at industry and partner events, which makes them the closest to on-the-ground sales-to-customer interactions.

Field marketing is responsible for: Sales-aligned activities driven at the local level to support that region in ways that are specific to its pipeline needs.

Primary inspection metric: Field marketing is focused on pipeline, as part of the one-team approach. More specifically, they are zeroed in on engaging key contacts within marquee accounts in order to facilitate in-person conversations with the sales teams.

At Snowflake, field marketing, ABM, and the SDRs are the three sales-facing teams. All three support sales directly, are aligned to their territories, and are mapped to their sales leaders. (As opposed to demand gen and partner marketing, both of whom support the company as a whole.) This makes cross-functional collaboration even easier since we've got alignment built into our team DNA.

How ABM Works with Field Marketing: ABM and field marketing do a lot of strategic consultation together. If field marketing is planning an event, ABM may pull data so we can collaboratively decide which topics and activities should be featured. Field marketing does the majority of agenda development, but ABM can also support them there.

When there are larger, corporate-level events on the calendar, field marketing will coordinate on-site events for a specific set of customers. They might have a manufacturing event one night, a healthcare event another night, and then a highly targeted event for just three specific accounts another night. ABM and the sales teams will help determine who from the company should attend that final, highly focused event, as well as get invites out ahead of time and work with the SDRs to do follow-up.

The SDR team may activate with field marketing around account-based events apart from ABM. SDRs may design events with them, help get invitees registered, and follow up on events in relation to specific accounts. When people have already attended a live event, that gives SDRs a fantastic reason to follow up and book individual appointments with those people.

We've noticed that some experts have shifted their language from account-based marketing to account-based everything, or ABX, to combine efforts with traditional field marketing. Those who champion this approach often say that field marketers can absorb the work of an ABM team while still continuing to perform their other duties. We feel strongly that this is a mistake. Field marketers handle an enormous amount of high-pressure work already, including event logistics and execution. Adding ABM duties to their lists inevitably means that content creation and prospecting get cast aside. Merging these two groups of work means that neither will get your marketing teams' full attention, but ABM is likely to get the short straw due to the longer-tail ROI vs. more directly calculable ROI from field marketing.

Example Play

The 3 x 3: One of our field marketing teams came up with the idea to host a three-part event entirely tailored to a single account for high-priority accounts chosen by regional vice presidents in sales. The entire agenda would be handcrafted for the individuals in that organization and the specific challenges they were facing, as well as Snowflake's solution to their challenges. Part 1 would feature a session led by our head of sales, generating excitement for what it means to be a part of Snowflake. Two weeks later, session 2 would be led by the sales engineering team, detailing technical specifics relevant to each group. Part 3, two weeks after that, would include breakout sessions across the buying committee to discuss everything from migration plans to product road maps. For one of these events, we had more than three hundred attendees from a single account. That's when we knew we were on to something.

Who you're talking to (personas): The sales team needs to be tied into every aspect of this activation, including identifying the personas. They should work with you to understand who the sponsors are, who the challengers are, who is likely to adopt first, and who the laggers are. For an account this large, they are expected to know the lay of the land.

What you're telling them (message): Because this is a hand-crafted experience, the messaging should be hyper-targeted not only for the account, but for different cohorts of invitees. The message to leadership should explain what they can expect to learn from it and what the agenda includes, while the message to technical experts should be tailored to the tactical outcomes they can expect from the events.

How you will communicate the message (content): The messages you decided upon above should be translated into both digital campaigns with touch points from display advertising, email signature banners, and custom home page personalizations as well as sequences from the SDRs and personal invitations from sales reps. You may choose to include a physical invitation that will be sent by mail to elevate the VIP experience. Consider creating enablement for internal champions in the account who can post to their intranet, send email invitations internally, or share in internal meetings. You will also need custom landing pages for registration and should consider a microsite/content experience dedicated to content from each of the three events that can be referenced throughout the play.

How you will deliver the message (SDR plays, marketing channels): Sales and SDRs need to carefully decide which relationships need to be handled by the account owner versus SDR based on which relationships already exist versus those that are new. Typically, sales will handle VP and above titles while SDRs will reach out to the senior director and below.

Timing: Timing should be guided by your sales team. They should provide insight as to when they have enough momentum built and relationships established in an account to make a program like this take off. If you do it too early, you can expect a lackluster response since not enough people know who you are. Specifically, you need to have a champion on your side who can help promote the series internally.

Goals: Targeted engagement with individuals across buying committees is key here. The goal is to connect with individuals you have not otherwise connected with and engage them in conversations with their sales teams.

Cross-Functional Collaboration with Partner Marketing

One of the core pillars of Snowflake Marketing is to build partner marketing that scales the reach of our marketing and create end-to-end solutions with our partners. This team is the one who nurtures the relationships your company has with other companies, and focuses on mutually beneficial activities. The work that they do transforms individual partner companies into an ecosystem of symbiotic relationships.

Partner marketing is responsible for: Marketing efforts executed *with and to* an ecosystem of partners, consultants, tech vendors, and anyone who resells or builds on your product, or sells something complementary to your product.

Primary inspection metric: KPIs vary by type of partner and activity, but at any given time they are looking to influence the pipeline and opportunities with a mix of partners and increase the scale of Snowflake marketing.

This team creates strategic marketing collaborations between your company and its partners to help both reach their respective business goals. Those goals might include increasing brand awareness and reach; generating more website and social media traffic; or growing your number of conversions. This strategy broadens reach for both partners and can also be a low-cost way to acquire new customers.

Partner organizations, especially consulting partners, thrive on building relationships across enterprise business units, so they have the ability to make introductions to C-level individuals in particular. This group can help get sales into the conversation.

ABM and the SDR team should consider tapping into partner marketing to supercharge and sharpen your plays to support sales. Collaborating with this team is a great way to develop new value propositions, easy access to vertical content, and new case studies and bring additional resources like training and enablement from partners for your own groups. At Snowflake, partner marketing has coordinated getting subject matter experts from our partner companies to come into Snowflake to provide validation to Snowflake's positioning and value to customers and train our reps on highly technical topics.

Typically, partners are eager to help you go to market better. Of course, they also have their own solution and their own angle that they want to push. When GTM teams cooperate with partner marketing, it's all about balancing needs and expectations. In addition, teaming up with partners also has to balance how customers may be at different stages of journey with different partner organizations.

Example Play

Partner Content Integration: While we have run successful end-to-end co-marketing one-team plays with partners, we actually find that integrating partner content and messaging into existing plays is the easiest fit for this relationship. There is one caveat that we stick to without exception: The request to include a partner has to be sales driven. This ensures that sales is fully engaged in the activation and that we do not unintentionally cause any political friction.

Quick caveat: Companies often feel an impulse to "co-prospect" with the partner's sales or SDR team. This means individuals from both your company and the partner are reaching out to the same set of accounts at the same time. While Snowflake relies on SDRs organized by accounts, many partners may have SDRs organized by geography. Thus it can be challenging to add value to the process while presenting multiple partner messages to the target customers.

Goals: Plan early to identify goals with partners. Engage with buying committee members that your partner organization has relationships with that you do not, and vice versa.

Who you're talking to (personas): Identify existing personas you are already targeting that are existing customers of your partner or could benefit from both solutions.

What you're telling them (message): Work with the sales team to understand how the partner offering uniquely accelerates the adoption of your technology. This could be a net-new deal or expansion to new features.

How you will communicate the message (content): Gather or create one to three co-branded pieces of content that speak to the joint value you add. We recommend including a joint-customer case study in this mix. Add these to your existing content experience you have set up for this set of accounts.

How you will deliver the message (SDR plays, marketing channels): Coordinate with sales, SDRs, and ABM around when the partner components should launch. You may want to run a co-branded digital campaign in parallel to your broader account campaign and integrate the co-branded content into one or two touches in your existing SDR touch patterns. Identify target titles and consider if you want sales to connect with VP and above contacts with a different touch point directly or invite them to a cohosted event.

Timing: Find a compelling event to wrap this play around. Whether your account(s) just signed a deal and need implementation help from the partner or you are cohosting an event you want to drive attendance to, this needs to be relevant and not random.

CROSS-SELLING AND UPSELLING

All of the tactics we've talked about in this book can be used to prospect for new customers, but many can also be used to foster relationship growth with current customers. This isn't exactly cross-functional marketing, but as an ABMer or SDR you become an extension of the sales team when you put your efforts toward upgrades and add-ons.

These tactics are critically important since maturing businesses increase growth mainly by cross-selling and upselling to their existing customer base, partially because acquiring new customers is more costly than keeping current ones.[1] It's also worth noting that 72 percent of salespeople who upsell and 74 percent who cross-sell say that it drives up to 30 percent of their revenue.[2] Clearly, these strategies work.

As an ABM/SDR team, one of the best ways to approach cross-selling (encouraging additional, related purchases) or upselling (encouraging upgrades) is to study customer usage patterns. What are they using today, what are they not using today, and where does it make sense to expand their usage? By introducing your current customers to solutions they didn't know you offered or features that would make their work even more efficient, you are helping them save time and money in a very direct way.

1   Gallo, Amy. "The Value of Keeping the Right Customers." *Harvard Business Review.* October 29, 2014. https://hbr.org/2014/10/the-value-of-keeping-the-right-customers.

2   Bernazzani, Sophia. "Cross-Selling and Upselling: The Ultimate Guide." Hubspot. September 14, 2022. https://blog.hubspot.com/sales/cross-selling.

You're also showing them that you know what they want and need and that you value their business. Wins all around.

Snowflake's net retention rate is 170 percent, which means our customers don't just renew, they consistently upgrade and add on. Our ABM/SDR team keeps cross-selling and upselling content and messaging at the ready at all times to ensure that rate stays impressively high. Since we already know how to speak to and sell to our segments, creating cross-selling and upselling messages is a natural extension of our other work. As you build your own ABM/SDR practice, you'll likely feel the same way. Once you've got the motion going, you can unlock a new level of scaling just by tending to the needs of your existing customer base.

Cross-Functional Collaboration with Product Marketing

This team is the one who translates dense research into marketing-ready collateral. They're the experts on your company's industry and its practitioners, which means they understand at a deep level what those people care about and how they think.

Product marketing is responsible for: defining the value proposition for your company's offerings and deciding how you talk about benefits, problems your product solves, personas, and the product itself. This group crystalizes expert knowledge into customer-ready talking points.

Primary inspection metric: new product/feature adoption, content consumption by sales and SDR teams, content consumption by customers

Product marketing supports sales in a significant way. We consider them to be the heart of the marketing organization, with others taking their messages out to the market, but also surfacing feedback and sending it back to the heart.

Snowflake's SDR team particularly benefits from collaboration with product marketing. Product marketing is the bridge, offering insight and messaging input that helps SDRs craft emails and outreach that truly resonate.

We value their input so much that we overhauled our SDR sequence library with product marketing as a key partner. We worked directly with them to define the spacing, timing, and type of messages we want to send. They helped Travis's team determine the right balance between a sprawl of one-off sequences and a small, controlled library to measure and optimize. Ultimately we landed on seventeen sequences that capture all the key ways that we communicate to our market.

However, we also find that relying solely on product marketing leads to messaging that's too lengthy and doesn't capture a human tone. We recommend that the ABM and SDR teams collaborate with product marketing, understand the key points they want you to mention, and then engage your sales development leader or tenured salespeople to transform and massage and distill those messages down to the point where they're super concise. What you get directly from product marketing might not make sense for a person to actually send out to another person. And that refinement process is something that a lot of companies ignore. It's actually key to translating strong core messaging into actionable and effective outreach and communication from your sales teams or your SDR team.

Example Play

Sales Play Bundles: Work with your product marketing organization to include GTM components of their enablement bundles. For example, if they are preparing collateral for sales that includes messaging, personas, and competitive cheat sheets for a specific solution, pair that with an SDR sequence, a direct mail piece, an ABM content library, and documented processes to activate all of them. When you bring these all together, you create a more direct path to activation in-market for accounts that fit the target audience for that solution.

Who you're talking to (personas): The personas should be defined by product marketing for the solution bundle/sales play they are crafting. Work with them to understand if there are nuances per title or if there are multiple personas per the one solution.

What you're telling them (message): The message you use should carry across the enablement and sales, SDR, and ABM touch points. The consistency of this message is what really makes the impact compared to disparate touch points and messages.

How you will communicate the message (content): Choose the channels that you have nailed down with clear SLAs. Since this bundle will be sent out to all of sales as a form of enablement, you need to be able to activate quickly and effectively with clear measurement of success. We recommend keeping this simple and including two or three assets. When you are ready to scale cross-functionally, consider including a field marketing event as well or even partner plays that can be activated.

How you will deliver the message (SDR plays, marketing channels): Include a minimum of an SDR sequence, AE emails to VP and above contacts, ABM content experience, and ABM digital display advertisements.

Timing: These pair well with product or feature launches.

Goals: Measure the number of targeted accounts with campaign responses, page visits, and meetings with SDRs and sales related to the solution you focused on.

INSIDE THE IGLOO WITH SNOWFLAKE:

Caitlin DeMartini, senior director of field marketing for North America and Latin America at Snowflake, on how cross-functional collaboration benefits everyone

Caitlin DeMartini, head of field marketing at Snowflake, got her start at the company as an SDR. She found early on that her dedication to partnering with sales to achieve their goals was a differentiating factor in her success compared to her peers. Noticed quickly by the marketing organization, Caitlin was quickly transitioned to field marketing, where she could continue to leverage those skills while building out the function from scratch. Today, she leads a team of seventeen field marketers who execute hundreds of field-aligned events per quarter.

We asked her to speak about the critical importance of cross-functional collaboration and how she's seen it strengthen a one-team GTM approach.

To me, the underlying purpose of cross-functional work is eliminating confusion. It helps reduce the risk factor of sales not paying attention to important variables and events. I think marketing can be pretty confusing to salespeople, especially if they don't have a background in it, or have had bad experiences collaborating with marketing in the past. With marketing teams working together, we can bring unified ideas, goals, and messages to sales.

I've found that the minds of salespeople are wired to focus on a few things at one time, so it's a bad idea to throw too many different things at them. A unified voice is always more powerful and stronger. The message that we're all trying to communicate to them and the actions that we're all asking them to take are all connected. And if we're all saying it in different ways, that's hard to follow. That's how you create confusion. But when we can all get on the same page around conveying that message—when we agree on how we're going to propose that sales take action—they're able to get on board and move forward.

Once that communication is clarified, it becomes critically important to set clear swim lanes for everyone involved. Both marketing and sales need to know how the collaboration will work. When you're cooperating across multiple teams you need to know what you're responsible for, what everyone else is responsible for, and when all of it is due. When two people or teams are not aligned, they may end up working on the same thing without realizing it. When their paths suddenly cross, that creates friction. That is damaging to a cross-functional relationship for sure.

Then, to ensure you can continue building successful cross-functional collaborations, be sure to celebrate your wins. It's important—especially for those of us in leadership positions—to highlight the cross-functional wins we all create. So I'm in field marketing, and if I see something that's being done really well by ABM, I should make sure that people know about it and share that story out. Not only does that create mindshare but it also boosts morale and boosts confidence. People want to be on winning teams, and they'll be eager to collaborate if they know their mutual wins will be recognized.

The examples we've provided in this chapter only scratch the surface of what is possible with a fully integrated one-team GTM motion. The true value of this motion is unlocked when you establish strong, trusting relationships with your cross-functional teams. Once other marketing groups know they can rely on each other to amplify their efforts and you show how willing you are to join forces, the possibilities are nearly infinite. You've moved even closer to embracing a one-team framework and creating programs, processes, and results that would be impossible for siloed, disconnected teams to achieve.

MINIMUM VIABLE CROSS-FUNCTIONAL COLLABORATION

Pick one other team that you want to make a motion with.

SCALED CROSS-FUNCTIONAL COLLABORATION

Have a clear play with each team, so you really are one big team.

MISTAKES TO AVOID

Don't make SDRs do work that can be done by computers.

Don't go to these teams without fully baked plans, previous successes, and hard data.

Don't compromise depth for breadth. You're better off going after one account in a meaningful way as opposed to all accounts together in a bad way.

12

Using Data to Bust Silos

Many chapters ago, we mentioned that ABM has surpassed its era of being overhyped and started to settle into being an accepted way of doing business. This means that more and more use cases are emerging and accepted as legitimate, while second- and third-generation products related to ABM are being created and released. In other words, account-based is no longer just a buzzy, trendy new set of tactics that businesses are toying with. It's been put through its paces, and proven as a marketing method that works reliably in B2B contexts.

So what's next? Data is at the heart of the next evolution of ABM and unlocks whole new levels of alignment for one-team GTM. Technology and data have advanced so rapidly in favor of ABM that we think the best is yet to come with fully realizing the value of this motion.

The current and emerging innovations we've seen will help you level up your silo-busting game. Now that you've transformed sales and marketing into one big, unified team, you're positioned to leverage tech to eradicate silos from your data. After all, if your teams are communicating but your data is still siloed, you're not fully aligned.

So let's talk about how you can push the bleeding edge of One-Team GTM using data.

Looking Forward in Your Account-Based Practice

It may be tempting to keep your focus on just creating and scaling your account-based practice, one step at a time, little by little. And, of course, you should do that to some extent. But we'd encourage you to layer some future-forward thinking on top of your building activities. What's your ultimate vision for one-team GTM within your company? What goes beyond the mechanisms you're putting in place right now? Employing this type of thinking helps you put best practices in place as you build. We think you should do that now, in the early days, since those best practices will become infrastructure, and emerging technologies will help you automate on top of that infrastructure later.

Here's how we imagine this unfolding for you: You've already determined how to bust your internal silos, create stellar content, and work as one big team. You know how many days should elapse between sequence touches, what type of messaging you need, and which types of ads work best. All of those become inputs. When you're ready to orchestrate and automate as new technology becomes available, you can put those inputs into those technologies.

You can tell your systems to include certain messaging or show a particular ad every time it encounters someone from a certain persona about a specific topic, when intent is high for that topic. If someone gets added to your database with a certain job title, they'll get put into a predetermined sequence that you set up already, then trigger the creation of complementary, person-focused content experience, unique direct mail based on their interests, and person-specific advertisements. If you know that every three days is the perfect cadence for one type of communication, you'll have tools that can execute outreach or specific touches every three days without fail.

All that said, we don't think one-team GTM will ever become a practice that can be run entirely without human input and oversight. After all, it's centered around customization, personalization, and speaking directly to the needs of your customers. To understand those things, you need people focused on customers.

Real Customer-Centricity Requires Unified Data

It's becoming harder to differentiate between authentic, informational messaging and marketing noise. As AI bots begin to generate more of the content we consume, we human marketers are challenged to do what the machines cannot: focus on the customer. We need to be product-driven and value-driven in ways that AI can't emulate. Building relationship trust by listening and responding, understanding what customers need, and offering it to them as directly as possible: These strategies will become mandatory as the world gets overloaded with promotional messages of all kinds.

Account-based strategies can power customer-centricity in near-infinite ways. What you've just learned equips you to create campaigns that speak directly to your customers and serve their most pressing needs.

Many companies claim to be customer-driven yet struggle to deliver on their promise. By embracing a unified account-based approach, you've got an instant advantage: one-team GTM is customer-driven by its very nature. Simply by tailoring messages to customer needs, reaching out to individuals who have actively expressed interest in your offerings, and supporting people in solving their problems, you're putting customers at the center. It's labor-intensive work that can never be fully automated, because it requires listening skills, intuition, rapport, and human collaboration. One-team GTM is an approach that requires genuine customer-centricity of everyone who practices it.

Catalyzing relevant conversations will always be part of the unified account-based approach, and you can't have relevant conversations without data. Especially at scale. Throughout this book we've talked about multiple ways to collect, categorize, and leverage data from first- and third-party sources. But in order to do this really well at scale—and especially to use data and data-driven customer interactions to continually grow a business—you need all of that data in one place so you can take action on it in a truly intelligent way. And Snowflake is the place where all of that comes together.

Snowflake's platform enables different use cases across the business to operate in unison. And when you migrate to the data cloud, it won't just be marketing and sales silos you're busting. Our solution makes it possible for everyone in your company to collaborate and build on your shared data, fostering new interdepartmental partnerships and leveling up existing ones.

With us, the customer-centricity you've cultivated in your one-team practice can become a company-wide competency.

Here's an example to show you what we mean.

Say someone from an account you're targeting RSVPs to a live event your company is hosting. Your customer data platform might tell you, "Great, this person is attending. We don't need to feed her any more data." But guess who hasn't received that crucial information automatically? Your customer data platform. Which means other marketing functions might still be running campaigns to that same person asking them to register for the event. Since different groups work with different systems and those systems don't talk to each other, you've got data latency. You've got lag. Your company is throwing ads and messages at this one person that accomplishes two bad things simultaneously: it costs you money and tarnishes their perception of your brand.

When you work with a data cloud solution, you can feed all your data sources into it regardless of where they're coming from. The processing is coming to your data, as opposed to your data having to be moved to the processing.

That allows you to create what we call a customer 360: a single view of all of your customer data organized, harmonized and ready to be acted upon. Basically, Snowflake empowers marketers to operate from a single source of truth across the organization and collaborate on data without the need to connect, copy, or move data between silos. It busts data silos just by existing, improving access to data and generating insights that drive marketing and improve the customer journey.

And yes, the two of us are slightly biased, but we've also worked at plenty of other companies and seen how frustrating it can be to build collaborative relationships when data and tools are spread across teams. Attempting to correlate, share, and make sense of advertising data, audience-building campaigns, engagement stats, and website visits when each working group is using different software is an unending nightmare. You can ask your engineering teams to stitch all of this data together and make sense of it, but doing that will be extremely expensive, complex, and time-consuming.

Plus this inherently disjointed way of working is increasingly inefficient, because every company is now a data company. Virtually all companies collect data on their customers' behaviors and use patterns and use that information to make important business decisions. The trouble is that data silos naturally emerge, fracturing the lens into customer insight and making it very difficult to unlock the power of data. Which is precisely why a data cloud platform is so important: It enables companies to break down these silos and consolidate data into a single source of truth.

And as a bonus, busting data silos is easier than ever before. Data operations are no longer the strict domain of IT or engineering. Sales and marketing teams are getting technical and tapping into the power of data warehouses, machine learning, and data science to enable their own work. The two of us happen to have been beaten by the lucky stick working in a company that leads this silo-busting movement, and we've seen firsthand the power of a solution like Snowflake in the hands of a GTM team.

We've also built our One-Team GTM practice with Snowflake at the center, and the platform itself has enabled us to create effective and innovative campaigns, one after another.

INSIDE THE IGLOO WITH SNOWFLAKE:

Matthew Los Kamp, marketing data science manager at Snowflake, on best practices for building predictive models

Matt leads Snowflake's marketing data science team. The team's work spans the full marketing funnel with a particular focus on inbound lead scoring, account propensity modeling, and pipeline forecasting. He has ten years of experience in B2B technology sales and marketing analytics. He holds a master's in data science from Northwestern University and bachelor of science in business administration from Bryant University.

We asked him to speak about Snowflake's pipeline forecasting models and offer some advice on creating helpful predictive models inside of growing companies.

Our pipeline forecasting model at Snowflake is different from most other companies. We've built a bottom-up model that uses all the individual components that impact our forecasts. We model this in two stages.

In the first stage we analyze our existing sales pipeline to determine the likelihood that currently open deals in the pipeline will still be in progress when we arrive at a future fiscal quarter. This gives us really granular insights into the timing of our open sales deals. We can actually look a quarter ahead and say, we think some of these deals are going to push from Q4 into Q1, or some of our Q2 deals might be accelerated forward based on a holistic understanding of the opportunity. That helps us understand how well positioned we are for future quarters and allows us to see where there might be gaps in our forecast.

The second stage is using our historical data to forecast how many new opportunities we expect to open up based on staffing and trends within each of our regions. So we can figure out between now and a given future quarter how many opportunities will be opened and when we expect those newly created opportunities to be forecasted to close by our sales team.

I should mention, too, that in each step in this modeling, determining the likelihood that an account will open a new opportunity with Snowflake, the likelihood that it will remain in forecast until the expected close quarter, and the likelihood we'll convert that opportunity, we need access to the full company's data. This type of model requires strong partnerships between all our GTM analytics teams. We need to access data from sales data science, finance data science, and product data science. If we want to put together that comprehensive picture of what our accounts look like and what our opportunities look like, we have to have full visibility.

If you're working in just your marketing silo and you don't have access to all the data across your other teams, it is incredibly complicated to put this together and would be a real pain. I know a lot of companies are facing that challenge. They can't access the data they need across different departments. That's something that Snowflake makes incredibly easy for us to do.

But you can definitely begin the data modeling process even if you aren't a Snowflake customer. If you are starting at ground zero and want to build this type of model, the first thing that you need to do is ensure that your team is capturing good data. And it's not just about having an accurate picture of the world today, it's about building the processes to continually capture and catalog data over time. Our pipeline forecasting model is only possible because we have comprehensive snapshots of our data that allows us to re-create what our pipeline and accounts looked like at any point in the past several years.

I think that's where a lot of companies struggle: They don't invest in data engineering teams to build the data assets that enable prediction. If you don't—if you aren't saving all the information you can gather—you won't be able to build models in the future. The models will have nothing to learn from unless you have good data to train them on. I'd encourage teams to focus initially on making sure that they are capturing that data and building their foundational reporting on top of that. Exposing it back to the business is what is going to ensure that you're capturing clean data and the fields that are likely to be important for your modeling efforts. Then when you have your first data scientists they will be able to come in and really ramp up quickly.

I'll close by saying I don't think it's realistic to expect to go from zero to advanced modeling overnight. Even with Snowflake, you need to have that foundation of capturing data and building robust reporting. Starting there is your best path to success.

Cooperate, Communicate, Collaborate

Naturally, we'd love for every reader of this book to become a Snowflake customer so they can implement one-team GTM as effectively as possible, but we also know that's not feasible for everyone. And while building a killer account-based practice is much easier with a cloud platform, all it really requires is a few dedicated people: smart, driven people who share a fierce desire to align sales and marketing teams, create meticulously calibrated messages, and serve customers with care. Sales and marketing teams that work in synchrony can increase company success exponentially. We know because we've made it happen at Snowflake and taught others to make it happen within their own companies.

We know that you can achieve more by teaming up and sharing your brilliance. That busting silos is the one and only way to ensure that communication with customers is clear, personal, and relevant at all times.

By leveraging orchestrated processes and unified data, your account-based practice can become the engine that drives your company's revenue.

By accepting that sales and marketing work better as one big team, you can create cohesive B2B campaigns that make your customers feel seen and valued.

By cooperating, communicating, and collaborating—using the tactics and plays we've shared in these pages—you can ensure your company's future success.

Glossary

ABM: Account-based marketing is a methodology to prioritize marketing efforts on accounts with the highest revenue potential. While the execution of it can vary in scale from one-to-one to one-to-many, the goal remains to increase effectiveness and efficiency to drive revenue as one team.

AE (Account Executive): Salesperson responsible for selling to a specific account or set of accounts.

DM (District Manager): Sales leader responsible for a group of account executives by territory, industry, or segment.

GTM: A go-to-market (GTM) strategy is a plan that outlines how an organization can engage with customers to deliver their unique value proposition. GTM teams are responsible for executing the delivery together.

One-Team GTM: The unified, scaled strategy and execution of an account-based motion across GTM teams.

Pipeline: The total number of potential deals that have been qualified as viable selling opportunities by an AE, but have not yet been closed.

Pipeline coverage: A ratio used by the sales team to measure how much revenue is covered by the deals sitting in the pipeline compared to the new revenue target they need to hit. This is calculated by dividing the pipeline revenue over a certain period by the target new revenue for the same period.

Play: A defined series of tactics executed between ABM, SDRs, and sales to drive a specific outcome within a target account.

RVP (Regional Vice President): Sales leader responsible for a group of accounts organized by territory, industry, or segment.

SDR: Sales development is a specialized function responsible for outbound prospecting and inbound lead qualification with the goal of generating sales meetings and pipeline. An SDR is a sales development representative. This role is also known as BDR, ADR, or LDR and can vary between specialized outbound, inbound, or "allbound" (owning both inbound and outbound for assigned accounts).

Appendix: Tiers of Plays at Snowflake

When we began our ABM practice, we started with one-to-one campaigns that supported whatever our sales reps told us they needed. The structure was mostly the same for any given account, with messaging and content curated to be relevant and personal. At that time, each AE was entitled to a total of ten one-to-one campaigns at any given time to be used however they saw fit. It was a pull mechanism, meaning no AEs were forced to use ABM. If they wanted the service, they had to engage and contribute.

This strategy was wildly successful in building up our industry-leading ABM team at the time, and we were able to build more than two thousand one-to-one campaigns with only five ABMers on the team. One of the elements that made it successful was having the right technology in place as the team grew to help maximize efficiency once the initial concept was proven out. Since we had content templated and activated in a content experience tool and a consistent bill of materials, we were able to do more than a typical five-person ABM team.

In order to begin scaling the practice, Hillary devised and introduced five different tiers of ABM programs and made them available to sales to meet their various needs. The tiers vary in tactics, time frame, target list size, and other variables. And just like we are advising you to do, she rolled them out one at a time, piloting, perfecting, then expanding as opposed to offering everything all at once. We'll describe each one in detail for you shortly.

But first, a note on tier names: Since our ABM team only had one offering at the start, naming was not a big deal. However, as we introduced additional tiers and tactics to the sales org, we found that confusion rose with complexity. One of our team members suggested we name each ABM program so that it could be more easily identified across the multiple marketing teams involved. And since we like to get snowy with our naming conventions here at Snowflake, the names are coordinated to relevant snow themes.

One-to-Many | Snowmobile

Campaign Overview: Snowmobile is the original program that proved the value of ABM and SDRs aligning in a single prospecting motion to support the sales team. This program is intended to identify accounts with active buying interest in specific topics in each region, and then secure a first meeting with them at scale. We started Snowmobile with a single region, and it became a global program that we report on quarterly.

This tier is aligned to the district manager (DM) level. We noticed that DMs typically had a specific topic or industry they wanted to pursue as a theme each quarter, but the accounts they targeted weren't necessarily as eager to talk to us as we were to them. Now with Snowmobile in place, we can approach the work two ways:

DMs can tell us which topics they are interested in—data science in healthcare accounts for example—and their ABM counterpart will come back with a list of accounts that are showing buying intent for that topic in that industry. This way, our efforts are better used with prospects who are actively looking for the solutions that we offer.

Or the ABM team can run buying intent reports filtered by a DM's region and identify possible themes for them to consider. The DM can then choose from the themes provided, and the ABMer will target the account list accordingly.

At the end of both processes, we end up with a list of fifty to two hundred accounts that are showing buying intent on a common topic. We can then target them as a cohort with consistent messaging, content, etc.

We don't stop there, though. While the Snowmobile program as a whole is organized by cohorts—meaning multiple accounts get the same messages—we use best-in-class technology to deliver one-to-one experiences when people visit the microsites we build. This means that while the base page may be curated for data science in healthcare accounts, as soon as the visitor is identified as belonging to a specific account, we further tailor the web copy, content, and CTAs based on what we know about that specific account. (Data-driven, as always.) This is an important tactic for maximizing the efficiency of the team while continuing to deliver meaningful, impactful, customer touch points.

Timing is everything for Snowmobile. From the timing of account selection to the timing of SDR follow-up, all touch points and activities are predetermined and orchestrated across teams. The ABM team aims to have the topic and account list selected prior to the quarter's start so that the first day of the quarter our initial group of digital activities can go live. Then, within about fourteen days of digital go-live, the SDRs begin their outreach to the same accounts with the same message. Meanwhile, ABM and field marketing are working together to amplify relevant, regional events to the specific accounts in the program.

In fact, we find that when ABM is targeting an account, that account is three times more likely to attend the event they register for compared to non-ABM accounts.

Campaign Components

Since Snowmobile is a one-to-many tier of activity, the campaign components are more like customizable templates than truly bespoke pieces of content.

Digital advertising with customized messaging per cohort

Custom microsite that includes assets chosen in tandem with DMs and AEs for the larger topic, CTAs to relevant events tailored on page load per account, customer stories, and an opportunity to book a meeting directly on their AE's calendar.

Thematic SDR sequences. Touch patterns that are highly integrated with the persona and target industry of the campaign. We also include e-gift components for coffee or lunch for meeting retention.

Participation in a direct-mail campaign designated for that quarter

Basic tech needed for this tier: Display advertising technology, email, CMS

Scaled tech needed for this tier: Personalization tool, content experience vendor, SDR sequencing tool

One-to-Few | Bobsled

Campaign Overview: Our one-to-few program arose as a variation of our one-to-many approach to meet a specific need of the business: product-specific plays. While you can activate one-to-few for other needs, we've mainly used it to address various segments simultaneously who have tech-stack nuances unique to bigger cohorts. Using one-to-few allows us to accommodate for those nuances at the segment-level while leveraging the scaled infrastructure of one-to-many.

We love working with our product marketing organization to get granular, product-related messaging to our top accounts, so we tried a list of fifteen to fifty accounts for various campaigns. Turns out, the ability to leverage existing processes and technologies in a new set of accounts works well, but more often than not, the list overlaps with accounts in our other tiers. When this happens, our one-to-few approach becomes a complementary talk track, building on engagement already in motion to deliver a specific message.

Another benefit of this program is that it enables us to give feedback to the product marketing org on what is resonating and what is not. One thing to note is that we only do this if sales is bought in on targeting their accounts with this message. No sales buy-in results in no inclusion of their account in the program.

Campaign Components

These closely mimic the components of Snowmobile, but on a smaller scale, across multiple segments. Ex: One larger play for a specific product we are pushing, with individual rubrics based on the below for segments that are using a competitor versus underusing the Snowflake tool they already have.

Digital advertising with customized messaging as a cohort

Custom microsite or incorporated content that includes assets chosen in tandem with the seller and product marketing for the larger topic, CTAs to relevant events, customer stories, and an opportunity to book a meeting directly on their AE's calendar. If an ABM campaign already exists, this content is incorporated into the account's existing page, as opposed to creating a new one.

ABSD: Highly customized SDR outreach that incorporates the same messaging and content delivered by marketing. This is orchestrated as an integrated function with existing talk tracks if the account is active in another ABM program.

Basic tech needed for this tier: Display advertising technology, email, CMS, database or product tool to identify tech stack for takeout/expansion

Scaled tech needed for this tier: Personalization tool, content experience vendor, SDR sequencing tool

Responsive | Flurry

The Flurry exemplifies everything we have shared to this point: identifying a problem, finding an effective solution, then replicating it across regions to become a global program. And while we aim to be proactive on most fronts, we also need to be adaptive and responsive when there is a business need.

One quarter, the SDR team pointed out that they were projecting a miss on their overall quota attainment. Since we always take a one-team approach, the ABM leadership team put our brains together to identify ways we could help. We decided to try making a list of all individuals that the SDRs had sequenced that quarter who had *not* converted to a meeting, and targeting their email addresses with a LinkedIn advertisement that pointed to a high-value gated asset like our top-performing Snowflake Dummies Guide.

The Flurry was born.

The program was named after, well, a snow flurry, where individuals are surrounded by Snowflake messaging. But here's what we love about it: the majority of the work has already been done throughout the quarter. In the final three weeks, it's our job to make a final push to ensure we have minimal waste in our efforts and get these folks across the line.

While we can't share exact metrics, we can tell you that the line chart for quota attainment had a visible hockey-stick uptick after we rolled this out. And what do we do when something works well? We scale it!

Campaign Components

Digital advertising with relevant CTA to gated asset (we love using LinkedIn for this because the form-info is pre-populated for the user)

High-value asset for solution selection

Basic tech needed for this tier: Display advertising technology with ability to target specific email addresses, email, CMS

Scaled tech needed for this tier: Personalization tool, content experience vendor, SDR sequencing tool

One-to-One | Snowball Fight

Campaign Overview: Modified from the original account-based approach at Snowflake, Snowball Fight was named after the idea of carefully crafting one nicely packed snowball and aiming it directly at your target. (In the kindest, most joy-filled way, of course.) This tier has always been aligned to the AE level. While AEs used to get ten one-to-one campaigns each, they now get between three and five depending on their region's breakdown of account needs. This number will continue to be flexible and evolve as Snowflake's needs change.

The accounts selected by AEs for Snowball Fight tier support can be their top three accounts in general, or any accounts that need some extra attention. The minimum requirement is that the AE must be willing to dedicate three months (one quarter) to the account campaign to be effective and contribute ongoing insights about the accounts in play.

Oftentimes, we find that the AE is already engaged in their top one or two accounts, so they may choose to use a Snowball Fight for their number three or four in ranking. In fact, we suggest that our sales team use this tier for accounts with already-open opportunities since that's where we see the greatest impact with this program. It allows us to use a one-to-one approach to accelerate their deals with highly targeted experiences across the buying committee. Meanwhile, our Snowmobile tier is very effective for opening new opportunities at a larger scale, so we lean on that for opportunity creation.

Campaign Components

The team pulls different levers based on the needs of the business, but in general these 1:1 experiences include:

Digital advertising with customized messaging per account

Custom one-pager that details how Snowflake can help them in relation to their current stack, industry, workload needs, etc.

Custom microsite that includes assets chosen in tandem with the seller, CTAs to relevant events, customer stories, and an opportunity to contact their rep.

Account-based SDR sequences. Touch patterns built for the SDR to specifically customize messaging to the account, with consistent marketing messaging layered in.

Customer stories. We use cases from other customers in the same region and industry for use in ABM and SDR touch points.

Participation in a direct-mail campaign designated for that quarter

Basic tech needed for this tier: Display advertising technology, email, CMS

Scaled tech needed for this tier: Personalization tool, content experience vendor, SDR sequencing tool

Highly Strategic One-to-One | SnowCat

Campaign Overview: As the most robust offering from our ABM team, SnowCat is reserved for must-win accounts, or "needle-movers" as our GVP of enterprise sales likes to call them. These accounts are selected by regional vice presidents of sales. Each RVP gets to select up to five accounts that will make or break their quota for the year. That's right, this is a full-year program. In order to make a serious impact, we need an entire calendar year to get into the depths of the account across subsidiaries and business units.

We find that the accounts best suited for this program are those that include more than ten subsidiaries, have some sort of momentum with our business already in play, yet have at least 80 percent of the account still unpenetrated. The goal then becomes to use the relationships we have in place to grow our footprint in the account.

This is the most-integrated tier with designated, one-to-one activities across field marketing, partner marketing, SDRs, ABM, and sales. In some global regions at Snowflake that are dedicated to net-new logo acquisition into new territories for the business, we have entire head counts dedicated to this tier alone.

The name SnowCat comes from the tractor-like snow vehicle used to travel across the landscape in the most treacherous winter conditions. We chose it because this tier is all about one team and one account, forging into new territory together.

Campaign Components

A SnowCat campaign has many arms that reach across multiple media over the course of rollout. These include:

Account mapping internally and from a third party as needed

Digital advertising targeting multiple subsidiaries and buying groups with customized messaging per group simultaneously.

This may encompass people-based advertising targeting specific buying group committees with tailored messaging just for them. (Side note: The reps love seeing the results of these.)

Custom one-pager that details how Snowflake can help the account in relation to their current stack, industry, workload needs, etc.

Custom microsite that includes assets chosen in tandem with the seller, CTAs to relevant events, customer stories (sometimes from another group in their own company), and an opportunity to contact their rep. In this tier, the page has a tab for each buying group with relevant experiences for each.

Account-based SDR sequences with touch patterns built for the SDR to specifically customize messaging to the account, and consistent marketing messaging layered in.

Custom direct-mailer campaign that amplifies the same messages being delivered via other channels

One-to-one field marketing events as needed. We call ours SnowCamps. They consist of a full-day agenda that has different components for different roles within the buying committee throughout the day.

Basic tech needed for this tier: Display advertising technology, email, content management system

Scaled tech needed for this tier: Personalization tool, people-based advertising vendor, content experience vendor, custom web-design resources, SDR sequencing tool, account mapping vendor

Acknowledgments

Hillary

The one-team approach extends far beyond marketing. This book would not be possible without the teams, personally and professionally, that enable projects of this scale to come to life.

To the ABM team: You have shown up consistently, ready to solve challenges with novel solutions daily. Your creativity, bias toward action, and leadership are the reason we can execute at the world-class level we do. A special thank you to Bre Gaul, Chris Marshall, and Andi Quilalang, the Snowflake ABM leadership team, who have fearlessly stepped up to navigate into uncharted territory. You truly make each other the best.

To the Snowflake marketing and sales leadership teams, Denise Persson, Lars Christensen, Lars Nilsson, Chris Degnan, John Sapone and Mark Fleming: Thank you for giving us the opportunity to think big, innovate quickly, and share our stories with the world. Our work is possible because of the alignment you champion, together with our teams.

To my cross-functional peers, namely Jackie Kiler, Caitlin Demartini, Jose Parr, Guan Wang, Tyrus Abram, and Matt Schreiber: Thank you for your collaboration in building the ABM/SDR function into what it is today. Your leadership across your respective functions has been critical to the one-team GTM approach we detail in this book.

To my mentors, especially my sister Marissa Dobbs: Thank you for consistently picking up the phone and guiding me through the leadership development needed to lead a team at this level. A special thank you to Tim Freestone for helping shape my approach to modern marketing and innovation-first leadership, much of which is reflected in this book.

To the writing and publishing teams: Thank you to Sally McGraw and Stephen Power for helping transform our complex ideas into consumable content. Your mentorship and support throughout this project extended far beyond the writing itself. Thank you to Michael Campbell and the Skyhorse publishing team for shepherding us through the publication process, start to finish.

To my husband, David: Thank you for supporting me in every way throughout this process. Whether trudging through long weekends and late nights writing or debating titles and cover designs, you have lifted me up and cheered me on every step of the way. A special nod to my parents as well, who taught me from a young age to be a builder, entrepreneur, and leader.

And finally, thank you to my coauthor, Travis Henry. While this book represents the incredible outcome of our work together, it is only possible because of the years of partnership and hard work that lead up to it. Thank you for believing in me and my vision, having the hard conversations, and continuing to think big with me. And thank you for being a true partner, exuding "one-team" in all that we do. Writing this book with you is one of my proudest career achievements.

Travis

One of the wonderful things about the technology industry is the willingness of others to lean in and offer guidance, mentorship, and direction. I have benefited directly from that culture of support and stand on the shoulders of many generous individuals as I write these words.

I first want to extend my gratitude to those who made this book a possibility. Thank you to Denise Persson, Lars Christensen, and the rest of the leadership team at Snowflake for believing in my ideas enough to sponsor the writing of this book. You've shown me what it means to truly bring out the best in your employees.

I also owe this opportunity to the longtime mentorship of Lars Nilsson. Thank you for believing in me when I didn't have much of a track record, and showing me exactly how far some "fire in the belly" could take me. You've been my constant advocate and pushed me to a place where I felt confident enough to publish a book like this.

Thank you to Sally McGraw, Stephen Power, Mike Campbell, and Skyhorse Publishing for taking my raw ideas and sharpening them into something worthy of the printing press. Your experience made all the difference in bringing this together.

I also could not have done this without my incredible family. To my wife Gentry, you're the well of motivation that I dip into when I am taking on anything that stretches me out of my comfort zone. You know me better than anyone in the world and exactly how to shake me out of my self-doubt. I love you. Thank you to my parents Lisa and Steve for always supporting me and demonstrating the importance of living your values.

Finally, a major thank you to my co-author Hillary. From the early days of building together at Snowflake, to navigating the waters of building a personal brand, to the gauntlet of writing a book, you are the best collaborator I could ask for. Your vision and passion inspire me to do better every day. Thank you for your partnership.

About the Authors

Hillary Carpio's entrepreneurial, competitive, and creative spirit developed in her early years while selling her family's farm-fresh eggs to her local community. For each dozen sold, she revealed a timid, seven-year-old grin, exchanged her chicken-imprinted business card and pictured the day she would be racing in the go-cart she was saving for. More importantly, she was learning how to create business experiences that not only generated profit but left meaningful, authentic impressions on her customers. Her small-town relationships combined with her passion for all things creative have fueled her passion for innovative, memorable marketing experiences.

Building on the buyer-centric principles she learned as a child entrepreneur, she intentionally focused her formal education on the psychology principles and creative tactics behind value-driven marketing. She later went on to conduct her postgraduate research in the peripheral route to persuasion. Her graduate work demonstrates how multiple, cohesive, highly relevant marketing touchpoints overcome a human's instinctual reaction to block out marketing messages and cut through the clutter of mass media.

Now a leader at one of the top tech companies in the heart of Silicon Valley, she is best known for her leadership and innovation in Account Based Marketing (ABM). She spearheaded the ABM function at Snowflake through its record-breaking IPO, creating multi-tiered strategies and integrated cross-functional processes to scale for hypergrowth. The scale at which her team operates individually and cross-functionally is otherwise uncharted in the ABM space. Her and her teams' unique ability to drive revenue impact through hyper-personal campaigns have been recognized by multiple industry awards.

In addition to her leadership role at Snowflake, her experience spans Fortune 1000 organizations, NetApp and Fortinet, as well as go-to-market advisory via VC's and startup advisory boards. She continues to share her thought leadership through industry conferences, events, and podcast appearances, including her own podcast, *GTM Speed Dial.*

She resides in the Silicon Valley with her husband, David, and spends most free time with power tools on DIY home projects. Hillary is a proud San Diego State Aztec.

Travis Henry is an expert in B2B revenue operations with over a decade of experience implementing top-of-funnel, pipeline generating strategies. He currently leads global operations for Snowflake's Sales Development function, including responsibility for organizational planning, sales process definition, technology stack design, and all enablement programming.

Previously, Travis led the consulting practice of SalesSource, where he built go-to-market strategies for some of software's fastest growing companies including Zoom, Procore, and Unity Technologies. He regularly speaks and writes about go-to-market strategy, and has been featured in notable publications such as *Sales Hacker*, *Tenbound*, and Gartner Research. He's been named a "Top RevOps Leader to Follow" by SetSail and won LeanData's "OpsStar of the Year" award in 2022.

In his free time, Travis advises startups and scale ups, invests in real estate, and gets outdoors as much as possible (usually on skis). Travis is a proud Cal Bear and lives in Denver, Colorado, with his wife Gentry and son Caleb.